My Story, My Song

Facets of Faith Through a Heart Warrior's Journey

Brynne Bish

First Print Edition, 2024
Printed in China

Publishing Services: Jodi Cowles, Brandon Janous, and Rachael Mitchell (Blue Hat Publishing)
Cover Design & Interior Layout: Tim Marshall (Blue Hat Publishing)
All photos courtesy of Brynne Bish
ISBN (print): 978-1-962674-02-7
ISBN (ebook): 978-1-962674-03-4

While the author has made every effort to provide accurate information at the time of publication, neither the publisher nor the author assumes any responsibility for errors or changes that occur after publication.

The lyrics of "Held" by Christa Nichole Wells are used by express permission of Weimarhymes Publishing, Inc.

All Scripture quotations are taken from the New King James Version®. Copyright ©1982 by Thomas Nelson. Used by permission. All rights reserved.

BLUE HAT
PUBLISHING
BOISE · KNOXVILLE · NASHVILLE · SEATTLE

This book is dedicated to all those who have passed from Hypoplastic Left Heart Syndrome.

May their memories live in our hearts forever.

God is Good,
All the time!

Contents

Preface

At the beginning of 2022, my life was perfect. I had married the man of my dreams, accepted a new corporate job, was looking to graduate in the coming year from law and business school, and had just found out I was pregnant. I likened this part of my life to the sweetest part of a symphony. The part where you can close your eyes and immerse yourself in nothing but the sound of melody and harmony dancing effortlessly in sync with each other. The rhythm of life was steady, and its pleasing sound led me to anticipate nothing but more blessings upon the horizon.

October 19th, 2022 is a day I will never forget. It was the day the symphony of bliss abruptly stopped. On a bleak, fall morning, the 20-week anatomy scan revealed the crushing news my son, Cillian, had a life-threatening disease. That day, my life fell apart.

As I witnessed what no mother should through my journey written in these pages, I wondered about the very essence of faith. I questioned God's goodness. I doubted His love for us when witnessing so much innocent suffering. And while I was thrust into this part of life unexpectedly, I learned that what can seem like a fracture of faith can actually be a facet of faith being made. At the very point I wanted to walk away from my relationship with my Creator, I turned towards His comforting arms. The lessons outlined in this book served once as my guideposts that not just led me back to my faith, but enriched it all the deeper than what it was before.

May you find words as a beacon of light guiding you back to the simple truth that will pull us out of the darkness: He is God. And He is good. All the time.

This is *my* story, this is *my* song.

Praying Through Suffering

Chapter 1

Namesake

"Before I formed you in the womb, I knew you." - Jeremiah 1:5

"Are you excited?" was the first thing I said to Sam the morning of October 19th, 2022. Today was the long anticipated discovery of whether we were having a boy or a girl.

"You have no idea!" Sam replied.

It was a dreary day in Cleveland. Pouring down rain and 34 degrees to be exact. But nothing could seemingly dampen our spirits, or so we thought.

"What are you thinking?" I asked Sam while waiting for the technician to enter the room. He replied, "A boy, I just feel it." We exchanged a smile.

"Okay, are you ready for the big day?" exclaimed the tech as she greeted us.

She progressed through the anatomy scan, assuring us that what she saw was good. "Femur size looks great, liver and kidneys are exactly how we need them to be, head circumference looks good!"

She moved to the heart and there she left a deafening silence that still echos in my memory to this day. One minute goes by. Two minutes go by. Three minutes go by. She says nothing.

"Okay, are you ready to find out the gender?" Her voice picked up.

Maybe it wasn't anything. *Calm down*, Brynne, I thought, coaching myself off the ledge.

"Congrats mom and dad, you are having a baby boy!"

My heart lifted. I glanced at Sam and saw a tear well up. I knew he was hoping for a boy.

"Alrighty. You two stay put. I am going to grab the doctor and he will be right in!"

I turned to Sam. "A boy!"

With all the confidence Sam looked at the sonogram photo and then turned his gaze towards me and peered deeply into my eyes.

"I think we should name him Cillian. I like the meaning."

We had kicked around boy and girl names for a while. We liked the sound of Cillian, but we loved the meaning of it even more. Cillian is Gaelic for "little warrior."

"Cillian Bish. I love it. Our little warrior." I smiled with the thought.

Thirty seconds later the doctor came in and pulled a seat up.

"Well congrats on being parents to a beautiful baby boy! Do you have a name yet?

"We do. His name is Cillian!"

"That's a lovely name!" But shortly after that burst of excitement, I saw his face slump into a sober expression. As his gaze drifted back up to meet mine, his eyes were filled with sorrow.

"I suspect Cillian has something called Hypoplastic Left Heart Syndrome. Basically, he's missing half of his heart."

Those words still ring in my memory, forever preserved as a moment in time that would permanently change our lives.

He proceeded to advise us to clear our schedules for the week. His last warning illustrated how severe this condition was before we would soon find out for ourselves.

"You are going to have to make some serious decisions, and rather quickly. I wish you the best of luck."

We made our calls, set up appointments for later that afternoon, and drove to the nearest Dunkin' Donuts® to sit and research the condition. At this point I was still ignorant as to the implications this diagnosis held. Throughout the appointment I was texting my twin brother who was in the medical field. He had been fast to respond until I sent one text. "I finally got the diagnosis name. It's called Hypoplastic Left Heart Syndrome. Do you know anything about the condition?"

I heard nothing. His silence served as a warning to the severity. *What is this?* I thought. *Is it really that serious?*

Sam grabbed a coffee, and with all the gumption I had, I typed in the words "Hypoplastic Left Heart Syndrome" into the Google search bar and hit enter.

"100% infant fatality. Open heart surgery. Low chance of survival."

As my eyes glided over those words, they instantly clouded over with hot tears that began to stream down my face. And there, in the Dunkin' Donuts®, I felt my spirit break and my heart shatter into a million pieces. It was here the symphony of my life shifted from the dreamy, blissful tune to a slow and somber ballad.

I called my brother. He picked up the phone at the first ring. I knew then his silence was him giving me time to discover what he had just found out.

"How much do you know?" he asked. "I know enough," I replied.

"Do you know about the surgeries?" With that question, I felt a little flame rekindle in my heart. A hopeful flute emerged on top of the somber ballad.

I Googled once again, "HLHS surgeries." In my research I found that while there was no cure, there was a series of three palliative open heart surgeries to work with the defect. These were some of the most complicated heart surgeries to be performed, and the risk of complication and death was high. But, if successful, these surgeries would essentially teach the body to survive on half of a heart. So, there was still hope. My eyes gravitated to two words I saw written over and over again:

Heart Warriors.

It was not a coincidence that just one hour before we knew of the strength Cillian was going to need to find, we named our son the Gaelic meaning for "little warrior." No, this was just the beginning of God penning Cillian's story illustrating His glory and providence, one that is written here in these pages.

Sam and I held hands and prayed, "Lord be with us." That was all we could muster at the time. And on that rainy cold day, Sam and I left the Dunkin' Donuts® with hands clasped and took the first steps down the journey that would test the limits of our faith, yet deepen our relationship with our Creator in more ways that we had ever experienced before.

Chapter 1 Devotional

Not My Will, But Yours

When I was 10 years old I was diagnosed with a genetic disorder called Spinal Muscular Atrophy. This is a progressive disease affecting the muscles. At the time, there was no treatment. Instead, I was told to hope for the best but to expect my bodily strength to decline over time. To what extent was unknown and would just be a waiting game. Hearing that as a 10 year old with their life ahead of them was devastating. For the majority of my childhood, I spent my life begging God to rid me of my disability, for healing. I so badly wanted to have a "normal" life, to not face the road I was tasked with going down that was riddled with unknowns. I lived every day in fear wondering when my body was going to take a turn for the worse, when I would lose the ability to walk, climb the stairs, when I would need a mobility device to function. Like so many who have prayed for Cillian's heart to be miraculously healed, I begged in a similar way for God to take this burden away and heal me. For years. And years.

But the healing I prayed for never came. And I struggled with that concept of praying to a God who loved me yet was making me go through this difficult journey. I tried to fill my mind with self-help mantras and books, but nothing answered the question I had for my Creator: "Why me, Lord? And why this?" So, I went to Him one day and prayed a simple prayer, "Lord, if there is a reason you created me to have SMA, I need you to show me."

In my eventual acceptance of my disability and limitations, I began to see how God can use a bad experience for good. Such was the motivation behind my former career as a mental health therapist specializing in chronically ill populations where I helped hundreds of kids accept their disability, and consequently themselves, in full.

Through deepening my relationship with my Creator, I have realized while it wasn't in His original design for me to have SMA, surrendering that to His will and trusting in Him has led to more blessing than I could have even imagined. Perhaps the greatest gift of all was one I had been searching for since my diagnosis: the ever-constant peace and true contentment in who I was designed to be, knowing I was loved and accepted by my Creator. My worth was no longer tied to the standards of this world, but to the One who created me and defined my purpose in this life.

Shortly after Cillian's diagnosis, Sam and I made our final trip home to Maryland before being tied to Boston for some time. Throughout that weekend, Sam and I had many people pray for and over us. Some even asked boldly that Cillian's heart defect be cured. This journey has certainly tested my prayer life in incredibly unique ways, and I have asked myself many questions that are common when experiencing trials: Why is this happening? What is God's plan and purpose through this?

Perhaps the most difficult question I have pondered is: if it isn't His will for Cillian to survive, how will I be able to see the blessing through the pain? I was totally lost on how to pray for this situation. Do I even bother praying for healing? Do I bother praying for Cillian to survive if it's not His will? Do I pray for my spirit to not harden and only that?

To answer these incredibly tough questions, I turned to the One who illustrated how to lean on faith through prayer: Jesus.

Throughout His lifetime Jesus prayed for many things:

1) Before and during important events that displayed His Power

Mark 7:31-35: Jesus healing a deaf and mute man
Again, departing from the region of Tyre and Sidon, He came through the midst of the region of Decapolis to the Sea of

Galilee. Then they brought to Him one who was deaf and had an impediment in his speech, and they begged Him to put His hand on him. And He took him aside from the multitude, and put His fingers in his ears, and He spat and touched his tongue. Then, looking up to heaven, He sighed, and said to him, "Ephphatha," that is, "Be opened."

Immediately his ears were opened, and the impediment of his tongue was loosed, and he spoke plainly.

John 11:40-44: Jesus raising Lazarus from the dead

Jesus said to her, "Did I not say to you that if you would believe you would see the glory of God?" Then they took away the stone from the place where the dead man was lying. And Jesus lifted up His eyes and said, "Father, I thank You that You have heard Me. And I know that You always hear Me, but because of the people who are standing by I said this, that they may believe that You sent Me." Now when He had said these things, He cried with a loud voice, "Lazarus, come forth!" And he who had died came out bound hand and foot with graveclothes, and his face was wrapped with a cloth. Jesus said to them, "Loose him, and let him go."

Matthew 14:22-23, 25-27: Jesus walking on water

Immediately Jesus made His disciples get into the boat and go before Him to the other side, while He sent the multitudes away. And when He had sent the multitudes away, He went up on the mountain by Himself to pray. Now when evening came, He was alone there.

Now in the fourth watch of the night Jesus went to them, walking on the sea. And when the disciples saw Him walking on the sea, they were troubled, saying, "It is a ghost!" And they cried out for fear. But immediately Jesus spoke to them, saying, "Be of good cheer! It is I; do not be afraid."

2) Jesus prayed in thanks and blessing

Matthew 14:18-19: When feeding the 5000

He said, "Bring them here to Me." Then He commanded the multitudes to sit down on the grass. And He took the five loaves and the two fish, and looking up to heaven, He blessed and broke and gave the loaves to the disciples; and the disciples gave to the multitudes.

Matthew 11:25: Giving thanks when teaching

At that time Jesus answered and said, "I thank You, Father, Lord of heaven and earth, that You have hidden these things from the wise and prudent and have revealed them to babes.

3) Jesus prayed for God's glory to shine through suffering

John 17: 1-5: Jesus Prays to be Glorified

Jesus spoke these words, lifted up His eyes to heaven, and said: "Father, the hour has come. Glorify Your Son, that Your Son also may glorify You, as You have given Him authority over all flesh, that He should give eternal life to as many as You have given Him. And this is eternal life, that they may know You, the only true God, and Jesus Christ whom You have sent. I have glorified You on the earth. I have finished the work which You have given Me to do. And now, O Father, glorify Me together with Yourself, with the glory which I had with You before the world was.

As the Son of God, Jesus' heart continually breaks with the heavy pain of those experiencing trials as they come to be. But many of us forget that as Jesus was human, He experienced every emotion we have felt, including the deep wells of grief. He also knows of the stress trials have on faith too, so much so Jesus Himself had requested to remove whatever burden He was facing at the time. As I continued to question how to pray through my suffering, I decided to turn to no better example than of the One who prayed through His own suffering, Jesus Christ. Jesus in His few hours left on earth spent His time in prayer.

Matthew 26:36-46 outlines His words:

Then Jesus came with them to a place called Gethsemane, and said to the disciples, "Sit here while I go and pray over there." And He took with Him Peter and the two sons of Zebedee, and He began to be sorrowful and deeply distressed. Then He said to them, "My soul is exceedingly sorrowful, even to death. Stay here and watch with Me."

He went a little farther and fell on His face, and prayed, saying, "O My Father, if it is possible, let this cup pass from Me; nevertheless, not as I will, but as You will."

Then He came to the disciples and found them sleeping, and said to Peter, "What! Could you not watch with Me one hour? Watch and pray, lest you enter into temptation. The spirit indeed is willing, but the flesh is weak."

Again, a second time, He went away and prayed, saying, "O My Father, [a]if this cup cannot pass away from Me unless I drink it, Your will be done."

And He came and found them asleep again, for their eyes were heavy.

So He left them, went away again, and prayed the third time, saying the same words.

As I poured over these verses, I began to see some themes unfold. Read the three verses above out loud (or to yourself if not in a group) to identify the statements made by Jesus reflecting each theme.

1) Jesus let Himself experience the deep wells of grief

Matthew 26:38 "…My soul is overwhelmed with sorrow, even to death…"

2) Jesus made His requests known

Matthew 26:39, 42 "...My Father, if it is possible, let this cup pass from Me...He went away a second time and prayed, "My Father, if this cup cannot pass away from Me unless I drink it... So He left them and went away again, and prayed the third time, saying the same words."

3) Jesus submits to God's will

Matthew 26:39,42 "...not as I will, but as You will... Your will be done."

In studying Jesus' prayer life, we have learned how to pray through suffering by:

    1) letting ourselves share our grief with the Father;

    2) making our requests known; and

    3) submitting to His will.

Therein lies the purpose of prayer: for His will, not ours to be ever present in our lives and our relationship with our Creator to grow and deepen as a result.

Reflection:

1) Are there circumstances in your own life preventing you from submitting to His will? Do they cause fear, anger, or bitterness? Whatever the answer may be, lay it all in front of the Lord and ask Him to work on that part of your heart.

_____

_____

_____

_____

_____

_____

_____

_____

_____

_____

_____

_____

_____

_____

2) As you have prayed this prayer, what have you noticed about your own relationship with God and your faith?

_____

_____

_____

_____

_____

_____

_____

_____

_____

_____

_____

_____

_____

_____

Understanding God's Will Through Suffering

Chapter 2

Bob Ross

"For it is God who works in you both to will and to do for His good pleasure" - Philippians 2:13

I've always been a big fan of Bob Ross. I mean, who isn't? The thing that interests me about Bob's work is that he will dance around a painting placing broad strokes of various colors with such confidence and intentionality. While his vision is clear to him, it rarely is to his viewers until the last few seconds. Throughout the process, without fail, I scratch my head wondering what he is up to until the end. And then, a beautiful masterpiece is revealed, one far greater than what I could have dreamt of myself.

Much of this journey was like watching a Bob Ross painting episode. I see now the beautiful masterpiece God has created through this tragedy. But in the beginning, all I saw was random brush strokes of various colors bleeding together.

As promised, Sam and I had a slew of appointments right after we left Dunkin' Donuts® the morning we received the diagnosis. We headed to our first appointment with a cardiologist at Cleveland Clinic to get an echocardiogram to measure the severity of Cillian's defect.

We learned several things from our first of many cardiology appointments. HLHS affects the left ventricle of the heart and can range in severity. Some kids have just a smaller left ventricle and others can have a left ventricle completely missing. What we saw from the scan was that Cillian had no left ventricle at all. It appeared the mitral valve which allows blood to enter the left ventricle and grow was completely sealed shut, like a door whose frame is welded together. The prognosis for a defect that severe was not good. Even with surgeries, we were promised complications. The more severe the defect, the higher the risk for those complications. We were also told to expect that these complications would bring developmental delays and cognitive impairment.

After learning more about the HLHS condition, we were advised that parents with a diagnosis like this can pursue one of three options. The first was compassionate care in which we would let Cillian pass away naturally. I remember gently placing my hand on my belly as I pondered that option. He immediately kicked my hand right as it was placed. "No," I thought at the moment, "There's too much fight in him."

The second option was to abort the pregnancy. This was a common path many parents pursued, but one that wasn't even a consideration for Sam and me.

The third was to pursue the three open heart surgeries. As we learned more from the cardiologist, we found out that the palliative open-heart surgeries came in three stages. Stage 1, or the "Norwood" operation, is performed within the first week of life and would be the most complicated procedure only yielding an average of a 45-75% survival rate, depending on the institution. The "interstage period," or the period of time in between the Stage 1 and Stage 2 operations, posed the most risk to infants for life-threatening problems. Many families are never able to leave the hospital, but those that do are able to enter into the "Home Monitoring Program" to allow patients to reside in the comfort of their home while they await the Stage 2 Glenn operation. Once the child reaches around six months old, they are able to get to the Stage 2 operation called the "Glenn," which lessens the threat of immediate death or serious complications to occur. The final operation, Stage 3 "Fontan," was typically performed at around 2-3 years of age. In that time of learning, we were also warned only 40% of kids who survive these surgeries make it to their 4th birthday, with many requiring heart transplants later on in life.

Sam and I went home with our heads swirling with this information. But despite that, one thing was clear. We both wanted to go down the surgical route.

This was a heavy decision. We knew that it wasn't a matter of if there would be a complication, but when. The question then became where we wanted these complications to happen. In the days to come we prayed for one thing: for Him to show us where to go making it so obvious there was no room for doubt as to where we needed to go.

Later in the day my brother called and asked me the oddest thing, "Would you consider pursuing surgery at Boston Children's? In my research they seem to be the best in this field."

We were willing to consider anything. On the one hand, a move to Boston at this time seemed far-fetched, as I was finishing up my last year of law school in Ohio. On the other hand, this was not totally far fetched. Just six months prior, I had recently accepted a job in none other than Boston, Massachusetts. This wasn't any other job, this was a job born out of an odd connection I had made during my disability advocacy work three years prior. Now, while it wasn't a crazy idea to move a few weeks before I started that job the following fall, it was crazy to move in the middle of my law school semester halfway through my pregnancy.

The next day a mentor of mine connected me with a pediatric cardiologist who asked, "Do you have the option of going to Boston Children's? If you do, that's where I would go."

Okay, this is looking less and less like a coincidence, I thought, *but still, it's a crazy idea.*

Shortly after that phone call I decided to take a break and opened up my phone. I saw an Instagram message from a fellow Heart Warrior mom who recently pursued three surgeries at Boston Children's. She said a few words that triggered my serious investigation into the possibility of moving to the area. "Hey mama, I moved across the country to Boston Children's. They specialize in these surgeries and it is the best place to go. If you have the opportunity to go there, I would seize it."

Even with these "odd" coincidences, I was doubtful they would agree to take on a new patient so quickly. I called the clinic coordinator who was referred to me by a contact in Boston and left a message.

After taking another break I returned to my computer to find an email from the clinic coordinator. "We have an opening in two days. Are you and your husband able to come in for an evaluation to talk options?"

This seemed to seal the deal.

"How do you feel about going to Boston?" I asked Sam.

"Let's do it," he replied without skipping a beat.

So it was off to Boston for the Bishes. Another brush stroke on the canvas.

Sam and I prepped our list of questions for the team on our flight over to Boston. Two days into the diagnosis, I already perceived the world differently. I saw things I would have previously overlooked. Sam and I saw a young mom running around with her 3 year old to get her energy out before the flight. Would Cillian live to be that old? We saw a young family of six going on vacation. Would Sam and I be able to have the large family we had always wanted? As I soaked up these images, I processed them through the filter of my new reality. And my heart broke. Over and over again.

Sam and I hadn't slept for close to 48 hours, so I was looking forward to the flight for much-needed sleep. But when I buckled in, I turned my head and tears once again poured out of me. It felt like my grief was never ending. We were exhausted, heartbroken, and lost. Even when our bodies begged for sleep, if it wasn't the planning and research keeping us up, it was the stress and anxiety of hoping Cillian would survive the Staged operations. I felt Sam and I had been tossed overboard, and we were drowning.

I put on some music. Christmas was fast approaching so I turned on a playlist of carols as a desperate attempt to lighten my heart, if even just a little.

I related to Mary's journey. The war within my heart was unbearable. While I felt this was the beginning of a long journey Sam and I were meant to go down, one ordained by God, I also saw the sheer impracticality of coordinating a move to Boston in less than two months. This meant finding housing, getting out of our lease, scheduling movers, coordinating a transfer of intensive prenatal care to another institution, all while attending at least three doctor's appointments a week. At the time Sam was working full time, and I was attending my last semester of law school with a maxed credit schedule. But above all of that, I was consumed with fear that Sam and I were going to be completely alone. This was terrifying as newlyweds only seven months into our marriage.

Just then, I saw my husband talking to our seatmate. I collected my composure and introduced myself.

Her name was Dale, and she continued to talk about how she was returning to Boston after visiting her daughter, who went to school in Washington DC.

"So, what is bringing you two to Boston?" she asked.

This is a very natural thing to ask someone you meet in an airport so Sam and I had received this question quite often. We would often reply by saying "Just going for a quick visit" to spare those who inquired the long story. Sam and I looked at each other and spoke in ways only couples can. *Do we tell her?* I communicated with my eyes to Sam. *Why not?* he replied in a gaze.

"We found out two days ago our son has only half a heart. He needs at least three open heart surgeries to gain a chance to survive, the first one happening within the first week of life. We are thinking about relocating to Boston to seek treatment, so we are checking out the facilities."

I saw tears well up.

"I never do this, but I'm touched by your story. My name is Dale, and I am here for anything you need. I'm serious. Anything at all."

She pulled out an old receipt and scribbled down her phone number.

Sam and I consulted with each other after our departure and said "Well that is the sweetest woman we have met," thinking her gesture to give out her number was out of pity, or sympathy at its best. Little did we know that through Dale, God was placing another brush stroke on the canvas.

Sam and I anxiously arrived at Boston Children's the next morning at 6:00am. Sam could tell I was incredibly nervous about what the specialists would find. We stepped out of the Uber and stood before the "Boston Children's Hospital" sign, just staring. We both looked up at the tall building, standing side by side with hands clasped. We saw the lights in the hospital rooms which came with a foreboding feeling that we would soon reside in the same rooms in the coming months. Sam turned to me and uttered a simple prayer.

"Lord, if you want us here, give us complete assurance. Make it so that we have no doubts this is the place we need to be."

Hand in hand, we entered the doors of Boston Children's for the first time.

When we met with the team at Boston Children's we felt our first glimmer of hope. This was by far the most informative meeting we had had with any cardiology team. In meeting with them, we learned there was nothing about this process that would help us determine how well or how poorly Cillian would do. This field is still relatively new and a child's recovery success is impacted by many different factors. We knew Cillian's defect was on the more severe side, so we were warned recovery would be a bumpy road. We also learned that while the surgeries are improving, many with this condition experience a shortened lifespan.

From our first interaction, I had this deep feeling this team was composed of people I could trust implicitly. Apart from our subjective feelings, it was clear Boston's was cutting edge. Their program was the most comprehensive we had seen, with neurodevelopmental specialists, top-tier nursing, and skilled surgeons specializing in congenital heart defects.

The team left us with one piece of advice to stick to before Cillian was born: relax. Take a vacation if you can. They informed us most birthing experiences are sprints of energy, whereas this was like prepping for a long-distance marathon we didn't train for. This experience would test us in every domain: emotionally, physically, spiritually, and mentally. As we came to find out, the team wasn't lying. The more I researched, the more I found out just how hard this road was going to be. In fact, HLHS parents have actually coined it, "the year from hell."

Sam and I left the long day of appointments, tired and with our heads spinning. We left the appointment asking the same question the team had asked. Based on the severity of Cillian's defect, it wasn't a matter of if there was a complication but when. So we asked ourselves, "Where do we want complications to occur?" After that day, it was without a doubt that the answer lay within that institution. This was where we needed to be.

Another brush stroke on the canvas.

And so, we moved to Boston.

Chapter 2 Devotional

It Is Well

Horatio Spafford was at the peak of his success in 1870. A prominent lawyer and partner at his firm, he was abundant in wealth and notoriety. Horatio loved being a father to his four young daughters, whom he doted upon at every chance. His wife, Anna, was a fierce believer in Christ and encouraged Horatio to constantly deepen his faith in God.

Things seemed to be going just right for Horatio. However, in the fall of 1871, Horatio would begin living what many would consider a real-life nightmare. Dry conditions and gusty wind sparked a fire that spread throughout Chicago, known as the Great Chicago Fire, which consumed his entire investment of property he had purchased just six months earlier. This investment contained the majority of his wealth at the time.

Two years after the fire, he planned a family trip to Europe to meet up with his friend and missionary he financially supported, Dwight L. Moody. Tied up in work, he sent his wife and four daughters ahead on the Ville du Havre ship with the intent of meeting them after his work obligations ended. While on their journey, they struck an iron sailing vessel and the ship sank. Eyewitness accounts recount Anna's calm presence to passengers, saying repeatedly "Don't be afraid. The sea is His, and He made it" while she cradled her 18 month old in her arms to keep her warm. Anna was found buoyed on a plank, nearly unconscious. Their four daughters died in the wreck. She sent Horatio a simple message: "Saved alone."

Horatio had every right to curse God, to shake his fist to the One who could have stopped the tragedy. But he did the unspeakable. As Horatio was traveling over to console his wife after the tragedy, in the very spot he lost his four daughters, he penned a song all too familiar to us:

"When peace like a river attendeth my way
When sorrows like sea billows roll
Whatever my lot, Thou hast taught me to say
It is well, it is well with my soul

Though Satan should buffet, though trials should come
Let this blest assurance control
That Christ has regarded my helpless estate
And has shed His own blood for my soul
It is well with my soul

My sin, oh the bliss of this glorious thought
My sin, not in part, but the whole
Is nailed to the cross, and I bear it no more
Praise the Lord, praise the Lord, O my soul
It is well, it is well with my soul"[1]

In this tragedy, Horatio and his wife, Anna, turned towards their Creator. They leaned on His understanding and mercy as a beacon of light in the darkest of days. And in those moments of grief, they found their faith renewed and strengthened. Their faith in the One who gives and takes away never faltered. In Anna's grief she said, "God gave me four daughters. Now they have been taken from me. Someday I will understand." Anna testified that in the hardest parts of grief, she heard a small quiet voice uttering, "You were saved for a purpose."

Horatio and Anna left America and settled in Jerusalem for the remainder of their lives. They were blessed with three more children, one of whom passed away from scarlet fever. They would spend the rest of their lives ministering to the needy with their two surviving children. On Christmas Eve of 1925, their daughter

---

[1]"It Is Well With My Soul" Lyrics by Horatio Spafford (1871)
Music by Music by Philip P. Bliss (1876) Public Domain.

Bertha was on her way to sing Christmas carols in Bethlehem when she ran into a man with his pregnant wife going into labor. They both had traveled by donkey from the nearest hospital that was closed due to it being Christmas Eve. The woman died overnight and the father pleaded for Bertha to take care of his child. Bertha recounts, "Here before me stood a rustic Madonna and babe, and, similar to Mary's plight, there was no place for them to stay." Bertha was moved by this experience to begin the first ever orphanage in Jerusalem. This would later turn into the Spafford Children's Hospital, which is still in existence today.

For nearly 80 years the Spafford Children's Hospital has provided holistic care to children throughout the Middle East. Because of the Spaffords' faithfulness to the Lord and believing beyond what the eye can see, the tragedy of loss in four lives led that family to bless thousands of children with homes and the medical care they needed for nearly a century.

Back in Chicago, Dwight Moody and his colleagues began ministering to those left homeless as a result of the fire. Later on, Moody Bible Institute was planted in the very spot where Horatio's investment burned to the ground. Here, thousands of ministers have been ordained to preach the good news of salvation throughout the world, leading millions to Christ.

"God gave me four daughters. Now they have been taken from me. Someday I will understand." I believe she does. And I think we can all learn from this miraculous story about the trust God commands us to have in Him. We will become people who, despite tragedy, begin to live out the words of that song. "It is well with my soul." No matter what.

I can only imagine that, in the middle of their loss and grief, Horatio and Anna were only seeing the colors splattered about on the canvas. Yet in the midst of tragedy, God was at work painting a beautiful picture of His blessing that abounds from a faithful heart, and steadfast presence through what seems like never-ending suffering.

Reflection:

1) What have you learned about faith through suffering through this story?

_____

_____

_____

_____

_____

_____

_____

_____

_____

_____

_____

_____

_____

_____

2) In what ways have you experienced what seems like purposeless tragedy, only to find the mastery of God's plan revealed later on?

_____

_____

_____

_____

_____

_____

_____

_____

_____

_____

_____

_____

_____

_____

Seeing God's Providence Through Suffering

Chapter 3

It Just So Happens...

"Therefore, do not worry saying, 'What shall we eat?' or 'What shall we wear?' For...your heavenly Father knows that you need all these things. But seek first the kingdom of God and His righteousness, and all these things shall be added to you." - Matthew 6:31-33

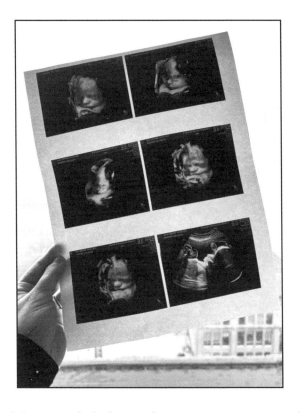

While Sam and I had tons of questions to answer, one thing was clear. We needed to move to Boston, and we needed to move soon. Speaking with the team, they wanted us to be in the area no later than 32 weeks pregnant should we experience complications.

Great, I thought, *ten weeks to plan a move.*

With Sam still working full time and my attending a full class schedule in law school, the pressure to orchestrate a move was growing with very little time to get it done. The somber symphony that had consumed my mind since the diagnosis was suddenly replaced with a jaunty, intense rhythm. Its pace quickened as the time before our move was running out.

We cleared our schedules once again, sat down, and collected our thoughts.

How are we going to get out of our lease in Cleveland?

Will my law school allow me to finish from Boston?

Will Sam's job allow him to continue working remotely?

How are we going to get all of our stuff to Boston?

Where are we going to live?

Where are we going to store the things we can't fit in temporay housing?

How do we prepare for hospital living?

When do we have a baby shower? What do we even request for the baby shower?

How can we afford Boston's cost of living?

How are we going to afford medical bills?

Are we going to be able to get all of this done in two months when we have to be in Boston?

Finding answers to these questions seemed like an impossibility. How could the details of this significant move be worked out in ten weeks? Yet we relied on the assurance in our hearts that God wanted us to be in Boston.

We opened up our checking account and looked at all we had: a measly $3,000. Sam and I had just gotten married five months prior, which consumed both of our savings. *Well, we at least have one month of rent covered in Boston,* I jokingly thought to myself.

We searched desperately for something affordable, accessible, and close to the hospital, but our efforts were futile.

We became so desperate, we started seriously considering opening a line of credit to pay for our stay. When I expressed this possibility, Sam said confidently, "We aren't taking out credit cards. Give God time to work."

Through his confidence, I was reminded of a childhood phrase my mother frequently said to us growing up, "Look at the birds, Brynne. They want for nothing. Who owns the sheep on the hill? Our Father in heaven owns the sheep on a thousand hills. How much greater He loves you than the sheep and the birds."

Weeks went by and we still weren't able to find anything. We were about one month away from moving to Boston with nowhere to go and the closest we could find to what we needed was a one bedroom Airbnb costing $3,500 per month. As I entertained the idea of securing the reservation, I still felt I was meant to wait and decidedly backed out of the purchase.

One evening I was speaking to an OB-GYN nurse about an upcoming appointment. Through our conversations she discovered that Sam served in the military.

"Did you say your husband was former military?" She perked up.

"Yes, that is correct!" I responded, wondering about her curiosity in the matter.

"And did I recall you saying you were having difficulty finding a place?" She said with rising enthusiasm.

"Yes." I replied, confused as to how Sam's military experience related to our housing difficulty.

"I want you to look up the Fisher House of Boston. They may be able to help."

I thanked her and eagerly hung up the phone to research the organization.

There on the website page, I saw their mission statement that mirrored the exact petition Sam and I were praying for, "Fisher House Boston's mission is to provide a home away from home where military families can stay, free of charge, while a loved one is receiving in-house treatment at any of our world-renowned medical centers in Boston."[2]

Free of charge? Yeah right. This can't be real, I thought to myself. I emailed anyway. Four days went by without hearing anything and on Thursday of that week I prayed, "Lord, if I don't hear anything by this Friday at 6pm I am going to book that Airbnb."

On Friday at 5:45pm my phone rang. It was the Fisher House of Boston.

"It just so happens we have a family moving out of our long term apartments, so we have a space for you and your husband." Sam and I were floored.

It just so happens. Hmm. Just like it just so happened I accepted a job in Boston, the exact city that happened to have the leading institution for these heart surgeries, six months prior? Perhaps.

We turned our attention to our jobs, both significant hurdles. I was slated to start the job in Boston the following year and Sam needed to continue his job in Cleveland until then to support us financially.

Sam reached out to his work, which was going through the process of moving people back into the office after the COVID shutdown.

"Well Sam, it just so happens that it has just been determined that IT personnel are allowed to stay fully remote. So pending HR relocation requirements, I don't see you working from Boston being a problem."

The seemingly odd "coincidences" kept rolling in, always in the phrase of "it just so happened." I let my future employer know the situation. "Well, it just so happens we are extending your moving benefits just a few months early to help with the move."

Remember the lady on the plane we met, Dale? She called me one evening in the same week. "So Brynne, it just so happens that

---

[2] www.fisherhouseboston.org

a food delivery service I order from is running a sweepstakes. The winner receives a $2,023 gift card in fresh farm to table food right to your door. I put your name in weeks ago, and well, you guys won."

It was here I began to see these odd occurrences were much larger than just coincidences. As I researched more about HLHS, I learned that a significant amount of pregnancies go undiagnosed prenatally because of a lack in specialized technicians who are able to recognize a malfunctioned heart. Many are born in hospitals not equipped with the knowledge, skill, or medical technology sufficient to immediately tend to their heart. Within hours, many HLHS babies pass away. I realized that if it wasn't for my having SMA, I wouldn't have been placed in a high-risk OB-GYN clinic, the very same clinic that follows those with a prenatal HLHS diagnosis. It just so happens I was getting a regular anatomy scan in that high risk clinic by a technician who was specialized enough to catch the diagnosis early, giving Sam and I enough time to prepare a move to the most specialized heart center in the world.

Of course, I saw these not as mere "coincidences." These were signs of God's providence answering the constant prayer we had from the beginning. And while I was just at the beginning of learning the meaning of God's providence, I began to see His providence is not in preventing the unimaginable, but in showing His presence and reflecting His power along the way. These were God's brushstrokes of color mixing together. And for the first time since we heard the diagnosis, I began to see the outline of His masterpiece at work.

Chapter 3 Devotional

Story of Ruth

It was an interesting time to have Cillian. I remember that particular year, around ten of my friends and family were also pregnant. While they were prepping their nurseries, I was prepping for a hospital stay. While many had homes with many rooms, Sam and I were packing our life into three suitcases wondering where in the country we were going to live. My heart was bitter. There were times I felt cursed. In this season, it was hard for me to want to recognize God's providence when we had so little, especially in consideration of others having more.

Until I read about Ruth.

For those unfamiliar with this book in the Bible, her story is not one to miss.

There once was a woman named Naomi. She had two sons who later took wives, Ruth and Orpah, to be their own. Shortly into their marriages, both Naomi's husband and her two sons died. At the time of their marriage, the land they were living in had a drought, forcing Naomi and her two daughters-in-law to relocate (Ruth 1:4-5). After pleading with them to depart from her, Orpah left, but Ruth would not leave her side (Ruth 1:11).

Naomi led Ruth to Bethlehem, where she once resided before moving to the land of Moab. When she arrived, the townsfolk who once knew her remarked, "Can this be Naomi [meaning 'pleasant']?" In her grief, she responded, "Call me Mara [meaning 'bitterness'] because the Almighty has dealt with me quite bitterly...Why call me Naomi? After all, the Lord has testified against me, and the Almighty has afflicted me." (Ruth 1:19-21)

Ruth sought out work to support herself and Naomi shortly after arriving in Bethlehem. Naomi had a relative named Boaz, a man of great wealth, with fields to harvest. It just so happened that the time of their arrival was at the beginning of the harvest season (Ruth 1:22). It just so happened that the fields Ruth first worked in were that of none other than Boaz (Ruth 2:3). It just so happened that at the time she was harvesting his field, he decided to "check in" with his workers while Ruth was present (Ruth 2:4-5). It just so happened that, of his expansive holdings, he decidedly visited the very part of his field in which Ruth was harvesting. Like Ruth, these unexplainable "just so happens" events kept occurring that were directing our feet to go to Boston.

Naomi's story continues. Boaz quickly fell in love with Ruth, not for her looks, which I am sure were apparent. He was captivated by her character and integrity, by her decision not to quickly remarry, by her loyalty and care for Naomi, and by her hard work (Ruth 2:11). And while Naomi was bitter in her grief, God was still painting His picture of providence through her tragedy.

You see, it just so happened that Boaz and Ruth would grandparent a man named Jesse who had a son named David. And through David the line would extend to Nathan, the father of Mary, the mother of Jesus (Ruth 4:14-22). And it was this child, Jesus, born from Mary, who would enter the world blameless to account for the sins of the world. It was this little babe who lay in a manager who would grow up to be wrongfully nailed to the cross on our behalf. And with every swing of the hammer that nailed Him to the cross, He saw the days past, today, and future days where His Creation was being crushed by the weight of sin. And He saw us even still being worthy enough to be saved by sacrificing His own life at the mere chance to be reunited with Him.

Had Naomi known in the midst of her suffering that the Messiah would come from her lineage, I wonder if her response to suffering in the present would have been different. I thought of this as I reflected on my own suffering throughout Cillian's journey. There were many days I felt cursed. There were many days I too felt I had lost God's favor upon me. Yet He was still weaving together

His tapestry of providence in ways that cannot be explained by sheer coincidence.

We had a choice in perceiving these events as coincidences, that it "just so happened," or that the Masterful Artist intentionally designed events as He meant them to be. That His design is so perfect, even the smallest of details do not go overlooked. For it is He who knows that, should one note be removed, the song would weaken. Should two colors mistakenly bleed together, the tone would change. Should a single stroke be made differently, it would diminish the power of the masterpiece He designed with such focused intention.

Reflection:

1) From a perspective of suffering, is there anything from Ruth's story that stands out and provides comfort in your own situation?

_____

_____

_____

_____

_____

_____

_____

_____

_____

_____

_____

_____

_____

2) Can you relate to Ruth's grief? How so?

_____

_____

_____

_____

_____

_____

_____

_____

_____

_____

_____

_____

_____

_____

_____

_____

Choosing Faith Over Fear Through Suffering

Chapter 4

You Are My Sunshine

"And we know that all things work together for good to those who love God, to those who are called according to His purpose." -Romans 8:28

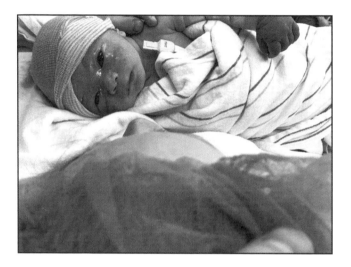

The time between us settling into Boston and Cillian's arrival felt like a timewarp. In many ways, the clock was moving incredibly slow. It felt much like the calm before the impending storm you see on the horizon barreling your way. Though it seems far away, you know you have limited time to batten down the hatches and get inside.

As a mother, I felt incredibly helpless. How does one prepare for a journey like this? The only thing I could think to do was to bring comfort to Cillian the only way I knew how: through song. Through much research I found that due to the extensive surgeries, some of these heart warriors go a prolonged amount of time without being held. I wanted to give something to Cillian so that he could feel grounded even without being touched, and had the idea to sing him the same song every day before bed so he would be able to recognize who I was in the time he wasn't able to be held. It's a song many of you are familiar with and one many who are reading this book have sung to their own children over the years, entitled *You Are My Sunshine*.

Cillian was born on February 15th, 2023 at 5:30pm. I was warned due to Cillian's heart condition that I wouldn't be able to have skin-to-skin contact once he was born. Because of his critical state, they needed to tend to him the minute he took his first breath. This was something I had mourned over, but fully understood.

But, all of a sudden they started cutting my robe. I looked to Sam.

"Why are they cutting my robe?" I asked nervously.

A nurse overheard and explained.

"The doctors think he is strong enough. Mom, you get to hold him!"

Tears welled up in my eyes. And before I knew it, there lay my little warrior in my arms. With beautiful big eyes just staring right into my soul. There are few moments in life when you feel time slow down. The 25 or so cardiac, NICU, and neonatology specialists in the room were all watching on standby, ready to place an IV and get medication flowing to help keep him alive. Nurses were chatting quietly with each other. Doctors were consulting with furrowed brows about next steps.

But for me, in that moment, time stood still. All the voices dimmed. I peered deeply into my little warrior's eyes knowing the long battle he would have to fight. In his eyes he returned not fear, not worry, but innocent love. In those few seconds before they took him away, I felt my world shift on its axis.

"Okay mom, we have to take him away." I snapped out of the moment as time sped back up.

The staff prepped him and wheeled him off to the Cardiac Intensive Care Unit (CICU).

And so, the journey began.

"I have good and bad news, which one do you want first?"

I loved Cillian's cardiology team. They were to the point, but also not too serious at just the right times. They stopped by the postpartum recovery room where I was staying shortly after I delivered when the lead cardiologist reviewed Cillian's current cardiac state with me.

"Start with the good, then go to the bad." I replied.

"The good news is there is nothing new to report and Cillian as of right now is stable. The bad news is for some reason he is over circulating pretty fast. This means he is getting more blood to the lungs then the rest of the body. We expect this in HLHS infants before they receive the Stage 1 Norwood operation, but Cillian started over circulating pretty much immediately after he was born. This means we are going to have to expedite his surgery two days from now."

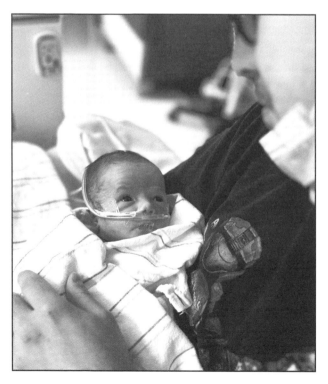

We held Cillian the entire night before his Stage 1 Norwood operation. Tears seemed to pour out of me no matter how hard I tried to hold them back. I had a million thoughts running through my mind, but one thought was repeated. *Are you safe to love? Do I allow myself to hope and dream for you?* As I held Cillian I was struck with the reality that this could be the last time. I felt my heart being stretched in two different directions. I had no control over the deep love I was feeling and it was wonderful and pure. While I wanted to dive right into this love, I knew the risk of it being taken away in a split second.

No, it wasn't safe. He wasn't safe to love. But he was worth loving nonetheless. He was worth every tear.

I tried to cement to memory the image of his unscarred chest. I watched as it rose and fell sporadically as he struggled to breathe. His hunger due to an empty stomach required for surgery the next day would wake him up every few minutes. As his discomfort grew, I would softly sing the comforting words he knew. I barely finished the last line in my head as his eyes fluttered back to sleep, unable to vocalize the words, *Lord, don't take my Cillian away.*

As I closed my eyes and reflected on that phrase that could so easily become my reality, I felt the warmth we exchanged with each other. Would the next time I held him be cold as I cradled his lifeless body in my arms? I placed my hand on his heart still beating. Would I soon remember this hello as also my goodbye? I hugged him a little tighter as the fear gripped my soul like a vice. A faint melody suddenly played in my mind as I ruminated on every thought and feeling. The sweet and melancholy tunes battled each other as the war in my heart continued. How I wanted to embrace this love, yet also run from the fear attached to the reality that it could all be taken away in just a few short hours.

I blinked and dawn began forming at 6:37am. I looked out of the hospital window and saw sunbeams peaking through the clouds onto the hospital.

"Go ahead and give him a kiss. We are going to take him back now."

I whispered in Cillian's ear, "Be strong, my little warrior."

And they wheeled him back.

At the top of the hour my family, joined by seven church families, two monasteries, and thousands of friends from 26 states and seven different countries, prayed for members of the surgical team by name. Since this was the first downtime we both had since Cillian was born three days prior, Sam and I actually fell asleep. And I awoke to our surgeon standing over me.

"A little tired?" he joked, "I am glad you got some sleep. I figured you would want to know how Cillian did." His smile assured me.

After a long explanation of the work he performed he said one phrase that made my heart sigh. "It was a clockwork operation with no complications."

Before seeing Cillian my family and I grasped hands and prayed thanksgiving and sang hymns. Sam's mom ended with one of my favorites which became my mantra.

"God is so good. He is so good. Yes, He is good, You're so good to me."

In that moment I memorialized that phrase to define the journey Cillian would go down. I knew God wasn't good because of the successful surgery. He wasn't good because of how He was redeeming Cillian's physical heart. He was good because of how He redeems the eternal heart through the good news of salvation. There is no fear in death with that truth. I understood that God's integrity remains constant in the good seasons and the bad. There were some days in Cillian's journey to come that would challenge the extent of that belief. There were other days where I would simply lean on that truth.

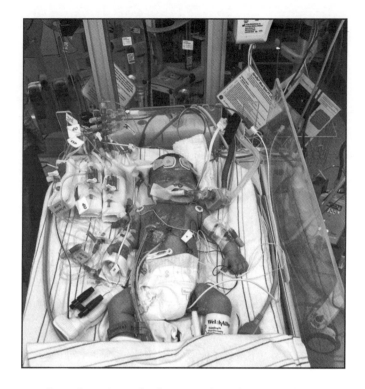

Cillian flew through the critical 48-hour window. It was difficult seeing him recover. There was discomfort and pain. It was unnatural for a mother to be robbed of the opportunity to comfort her newborn in pain. How I wished I could cradle his body instead of just touching his hand. The helplessness was unbearable. But even still, I leaned on the words of our song just as I did when I was pregnant. When he was safe. As he listened and recognized those words of comfort, his blood pressure would normalize, his heart rate would slow, and his breathing would soften. While this recovery was hard to see, it was nothing like the path that lay before us in the coming days.

February 28th marked 10 days from Cillian's Stage 1 Norwood operation; he was 13 days old. It was the first day I was able to hold him since his operation, but also the first day we experienced his first bout of issues. Sam and I were sitting in the back room sitting area. I looked at the clock, it was 12:30pm. Two minutes went by and we heard some alarms go off, not an incredibly unusual occurrence in the ICU. All of a sudden, someone closed the curtain.

Why did they do that? I thought worriedly. *Are we not supposed to see something?*

A minute went by until the curtain ripped back open to the image of Cillian's heart surgeon towering over us. I glanced behind him and saw a swarm of surgical doctors. I scanned his eyes for answers. His calming gaze reassured me, but the crowd of surgical doctors going through sterilizing procedure told me otherwise. The number of people grew by the minute.

"Anesthesia is going to meet you outside of the room for consent," he said in a hurried but professional tone. "We have to do an emergency chest reopening. A clip was placed on his shunt directing blood flow to the lungs and body during the Stage 1 Norwood operation. It seems that clip is tightening and he isn't getting enough blood flow to the lungs. I have to go back into his chest and take the clip off immediately. You will have to leave the room right now, but a nurse will get into contact with you about the operation."

We gathered our things trying to compartmentalize our swath of emotion. As we left the room, I glanced over at Cillian. All traces of his warm skin tone were replaced with a pale blue.

Shortly after his emergency chest reopening several odd things began to occur. Cillian's oxygen began to decline, he looked pale in the face, he wasn't eating as much by bottle, and he was overly tired. "Something is wrong," I told Sam and the team over and over again. The next day several pustules formed at the top of his incision. An infection had set in. Cillian continued to trend down that night. His bedside nurse called the NP's and ICU doctors into the room.

Cillian was listful and becoming difficult to arouse. "Try waking him up." One nurse suggested. She lightly shook his foot. She then stroked his cheek and touched his hand. No response. She looked at the infection, and the pustules had formed into big quarter-sized blisters that were bubbling above his skin over about one-third of his scar. She continued to lightly rock him. I could see the worry in their eyes, as Cillian was still not responding. Several more nurses entered the room prepping oxygen.

"Can I try something?" said another nurse. "Can we give him to mom to try to wake while we are prepping?"

Prepping for what? I thought anxiously. As the nurse handed Cillian to me I saw the team of nurses getting the oxygen ready. He flopped in my lap, nearly unconscious.

As I saw the effects of the infection quickly setting in I closed my eyes and sang to him our song. As the words flowed out I closed my eyes. *God,* I cried to Him, *please don't let this be how it ends. Wake Cillian up.*

I whispered the last phrase, please don't take my sunshine, as a plea to God. I opened my eyes to Cillian staring back. He had gone pale. I knew they were concerned, but our ability to get him to be alert was a good sign. Before I knew it, they scooped Cillian up from my arms and quickly placed him on the oxygen they had been prepping.

This infection would heal, but we had setbacks shortly after. Throughout the rest of Cillian's "interstage" period, the four months between the first and second scheduled surgeries, we were able to periodically bring him home. And while we soaked up every moment with him, he had to battle two cath procedures, nutritional challenges, sixteen daily medications, five admissions, and three emergency stays before getting to the second major open heart surgery, the Stage 2 Glenn operation. We didn't just have that newborn exhaustion, it was much worse than that. And while we soaked up every day of Cillian's "interstage" between surgeries, we were looking forward to his heart being stronger to shed some of these difficulties afforded to us by the Stage 2 operation. All with the same prayer: "Please don't take my sunshine away."

Little did we know that in the coming days, Cillian would have to face the largest battle of them all, one that threatened the answering of that prayer.

Chapter 4 Devotional

Turn Your Eyes

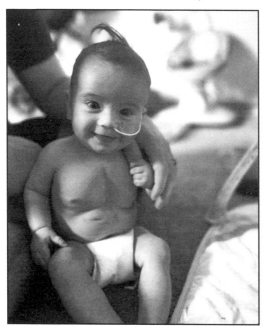

Helen Lemmel was an evangelical singer and writer in the late 1800's who traveled the world preaching the good news about Jesus. She contracted a disease that took her eyesight and almost her life. Her husband died very shortly after her recovery. Alone and lost in the dark, she remembered her favorite picture drawn by a woman named Lilias Trotter. It's a picture of a cold and bleak wooded winter. In the corner of the picture is a single daffodil whose radiance and color fills the whole page. It's facing the sun and is basking in all of its life and light. From her memory of that picture she wrote these words, a tune many of us have grown familiar with over the years.

"Oh soul, are you weary and troubled?
No light in the darkness you see?
There's light for a look at the Savior,
And life more abundant and free.
His word shall not fail you, He promised.
Believe Him and all will be well.
Then go to a world that is dying,
His perfect salvation to tell.
Turn your eyes upon Jesus,
Look full in His wonderful face!
And the things of this earth will grow strangely dim,
In the light of his glory and grace."[3]

Helen remarked that in her darkest moment this picture reminded her to fix her spiritual eyes to Jesus instead of looking at the all present and consuming fear.

I remember the statistics thrown at me on diagnosis day. Believe me, there was plenty to be afraid of, but above all were the mortality rates. Even with the Staged operations being successful, which alone held significant risk, there was still a 60% mortality rate of individuals with HLHS after 15 years of life.

At the time of diagnosis it was easier to look at the fear instead of turning to faith. But though fear continues to knock at my door, it is not given entry. Every day I have the choice to open the door, or simply recognize fear is knocking before turning my gaze to the One who calms the sea just by speaking its name.

Lillias Trotter put a quote with the daffodil picture she drew that inspired Helen's song:

"Take the very hardest thing in your life – the place of difficulty, outward or inward, and expect God to triumph gloriously in that very spot. Just there He can bring your soul into blossom."

---

[3]"Turn Your Eyes Upon Jesus" Music and lyrics by Helen Howarth Lemmel (1922). Public Domain.

Reflection:

1) Have there been times you have opened the door to fear instead of fixing your gaze on our Creator? What about the other way around? What have you learned from both choices?

_____

_____

_____

_____

_____

_____

_____

_____

_____

_____

_____

_____

_____

_____

2) What lyric struck you the most? Why?

_____

_____

_____

_____

_____

_____

_____

_____

_____

_____

_____

_____

_____

_____

_____

_____

Trusting God Through Suffering

Chapter 5

Held

It was 10:30am on August 7th, just one week shy of his six-month birthday. Cillian was well into his Stage 2 Glenn operation.

I always used long surgery days to carve out time and do what I love to do most and write. On that particular day I was aiming to finish the fourth, and what I thought was the final chapter of this book. As I finished typing the last word, I put on a 2000's Christian playlist. Though I was sitting in the community garden surrounded by lush greenery, it did not fully distract me from what was happening in the operating room just 500 feet away.

Then the strangest thing happened. The first song that played was one I hadn't heard in over ten years.

> "Two months is too little
> They let him go, they had no sudden healing"

I was instantly speechless. So many had prayed for the sudden healing this song speaks of that never came.

> "To think that providence would
> Take a child from his mother while she prays, is appalling."

My stomach tightened as I felt my heart break with each lyric. With those four lines alone, I knew the writer of this song was familiar with a similar journey to Sam and mine. Only a parent going through something so extreme would pose such lyrical questions. Time and time again I had found myself on my knees begging and pleading with God. And I wondered over and over what providence even meant to a Christian going through a journey like this.

> "Who told us we'd be rescued?
> What has changed, and why should we be saved from nightmares?
> We're asking why this happens to us who have died to live?
> It's unfair."

And then it hit. Like a ton of bricks. Hot tears streamed down my face. How perfectly these words illustrated the pain a mother's heart feels in a journey like this. There were many parts of Cillian's journey that felt like nothing short of a nightmare–the day we got his diagnosis, his infection, and the various emergency admissions and procedures. But part of me was wondering, was the worst of the nightmares yet to come? Was I meant to hear the words of this song at this exact time, right as things were looking to get better? Does providence mean healing? Being rescued from suffering? Does it mean God orchestrates a path for you to go down that is riddled with heartache? Is He a cruel God for doing so?

The song goes on.

"This hand is bitterness
We wanna taste it.
Let the hatred numb our sorrow."

My heart seemed to be ripped open even more with every lyric that fell upon my ears. I knew of the bitterness, the hatred, the resentment. I knew of the sorrow that shreds your soul. I remember one day in the CICU the babies on either side of Cillian's room coded. I have known stories during Cillian's time of kids and infants with HLHS dying. I have seen parents die inside from their child's passing and wondered to myself, *will that happen to me? When will it happen to me?* I have never wrestled more with the understanding of God's goodness.

"The wise hand opens slowly
To lilies of the valley and tomorrow.

This is what it means
To be held.
How it feels
When the sacred is torn from your life
And you survive.
This is what it is
To be loved.

And to know
That the promise was when everything fell
We'd be held.
If hope is born of suffering
If this is only the beginning
Can we not wait for one hour
Watching for our Savior?

This is what it means
To be held.
How it feels
When the sacred is torn from your life
And you survive.
This is what it is
To be loved.
And to know
That the promise was when everything fell
We'd be held."[4]

There was no more doubt as I finished the song. I knew in that moment that God was prepping my heart for something significant. Through the lyrics of this song alone, I felt everything inside me say, "Cling to these words."

Curious as to the story behind these words that so precisely reflected my own journey, I researched the meaning of the song. It was written by Christa Wells about her friend who had lost a child at two months old. After more digging, I was able to find the condition from which the child passed away–HLHS, the same diagnosis as Cillian.

There in the community garden, 500 feet away from the operating room and miles away from any degree of control over our situation, I had a premonition that these lyrics were meant to

---

[4] "Held" Words and Music by Christa Nichole Wells. © Weimarhymes Publishing, Inc.

fall on my ears at that exact time, though I hadn't even listened to the song since I was in high school. In a way I can't describe, I had a feeling these very words would come to be a lifeline in the days to come. And did they ever.

It was in that moment, and over the many days to come, that I grew a deeper meaning for what we call God's providence. There were many, including myself in the early stages of this journey, who mistakenly thought it was God's providence for the three of us to navigate this journey together. I then grew to understand God's providence to mean providing for us in a time of need, through the Fisher House of Boston, WECO, and other organizations extending their helping hand.

Through time and experience, I learned God's providence is even deeper than that understanding, but at the same time all the more simple. His providence is not for Cillian to have HLHS. It's not to have him go through pain. It is not for us to go through the trauma of witnessing Cillian fighting for his life at such a young age.

God's providence is also not limited to providing for our every need through a particular journey, no matter how difficult. In its purest, deepest, and simplest form, God's providence is for us to be held in the darkest nights born of sin's wrath. His promise is to be the one thing that elevates us just enough to keep from hitting the bottom. And while He cannot stop the effects of sin, He promises to love and protect us through it, even if just to be held.

The hope this lyricist speaks of only comes from salvation through Jesus by granting us eternal life beyond the grave, beyond the suffering. Christ heard and answered the earth's cry to be rescued from the effects of sin. And as He hung on the cross, He looked to the very day you experienced your darkest moments as a result of a fallen, sinful world. And He saw His role in suffering to be worth spending eternity with you. In our best and worst of days, His promise in this gift to us is ever-constant.

Chapter 5 Devotional

The Tunnel

The scariest day of my life was when we were discharged from the hospital after Cillian's recovery from his infection and Stage 1 Norwood operation. The medical staff prepared us for the worst. All parents are taught infant CPR and go through different emergency drills about what to do should certain things happen. While it is simply them doing their job, it feels like the staff are placing the fear of God in you. And then–they just let you go! As if you feel comfortable enough with the task of keeping your child alive in the interstage period.

Throughout this journey I constantly questioned, how will I be ready for tragedy if it comes my way? How will I be strong enough to prepare for the worst to happen? What if he does stop breathing or his heart stops beating?

The beginning of our interstage journey was going smoothly, when all of a sudden Cillian started to decline at a routine cardiology follow up appointment. Being so critical in interstage, these appointments typically involved getting a routine echocardiogram to check the structures of his heart and an outpatient visit with the team. Before undergoing the echo, we were taking Cillian's vitals, but were unable to get a good read on his oxygen. This wasn't uncommon, as the probes reading his oxygen are tricky to put on and manage. The assistant said, "No worries, we will just put the oxygen sensor on after his echo." We did the echo and Cillian screamed the whole time. We were used to frequent echos, but not Cillian's irritation with them. We did what the assistant recommended and put the probe back on afterwords. It was then we learned his oxygen had plummeted to a critically low level.

Sam and I chalked it up to the echo going poorly, but the nurse insisted we keep the probe on. After his levels were not recovering the team decided to admit us for monitoring with the full intent we go home the next morning when he recovered. He recovered overnight and was off oxygen right up until the moment we were being considered for discharge, then he dropped again. That marked the beginning of our investigation into why his oxygen levels were bouncing around so chaotically. Cillian continued to decline, and within a matter of two days he was completely dependent on oxygen. With no other plausible explanation, they decided to do a procedure called a catheterization, where they would explore parts of his heart for problem areas leading to his depletion of oxygen.

By the constant urging of the nurses, my mother, Sam, and I went out to eat at a restaurant to get a break. Though I was physically there, I felt like I was staring at life around me through a cage like a bird, desperate to get out. I saw a carefree couple out on a date not burdened with having a son in the hospital. I saw a young family out to dinner with friends, their arms filled with healthy babies and toddlers. And I reflected on those questions in the midst of not knowing why Cillian's sudden decline was occurring. What was going to happen? How bad was it going to get? Would I be able to find the strength to get through whatever it is? How would I know I am ready?

On that same day, I was reminded by a friend about the incredible life of Corrie ten Boom. She and her family risked their lives hiding Jewish families from the Nazi regime. Eventually caught, she was arrested and sent to a concentration camp. She recounts her time there in her book, *The Hiding Place*. And in the midst of the frigid air, with nothing to eat, witnessing her friends and family be tortured and die, she held church services. In the midst of what could be as close to hell on earth as anyone has ever experienced, she whispered praise to her Savior with the little strength she had left.

Corrie ten Boom would survive the concentration camps to live on, encouraging thousands to seek faith amongst tragedy. As I kissed Cillian before they wheeled him back to the cath procedure,

I was reminded a quote famously attributed to Corrie ten Boom: "When a train goes through a tunnel and it gets dark, you don't throw away the ticket and jump off. You sit and trust the engineer."

The cath procedure finished and we reviewed what discoveries the doctors had made. As it turned out, a splint from the Stage 1 Norwood operation had fractured, which was blocking blood flow from the heart to the lungs. The doctors suspected this splint had actually been fractured for some time and had only gotten worse enough to show serious symptoms while being admitted in the hospital.

In our pre-procedure consult with the cardiology team they said something that made me feel awestruck of the God I serve, the same God that inspired Corrie ten Boom's famed quote. "You know we wouldn't have caught this problem and gotten him oxygen support as quickly if the oxygen sensor wasn't on after his echo. It's impeccable timing." And I smiled. That's God's timing.

In that moment I realized God had humbly taught me the same lesson Corrie learned all those years ago. Don't hop off the train when the tunnel gets dark. Trust the engineer.

Reflection:

1) What lessons is God teaching you through suffering?

_____

_____

_____

_____

_____

_____

_____

_____

_____

_____

_____

_____

_____

_____

_____

_____

2) What lessons have you learned in past suffering?

_____

_____

_____

_____

_____

_____

_____

_____

_____

_____

_____

_____

_____

_____

_____

3) What is preventing you from trusting God through present suffering?

_____

_____

_____

_____

_____

_____

_____

_____

_____

_____

_____

_____

_____

_____

_____

4) How can you reconcile the above? Journal out your feelings by writing a letter to God and ending with a request for Him to work on that part of your heart.

_____

_____

_____

_____

_____

_____

_____

_____

_____

_____

_____

_____

_____

_____

_____

_____

Seeing God's Glory Through Suffering

Chapter 6

The Crucible

"But they who wait for the Lord shall renew their strength; they shall mount up with wings like eagles; they shall run and not be weary; they shall walk and not faint." - Isaiah 40:31

One of the things I have discovered I love most about Sam throughout this journey is how calm and optimistic he is in the midst of what can seem like pure chaos. When I am at my weakest, he turns to me and says, "We need to keep going." I asked him once how he is this calm when it feels like our lives are falling apart and he just said, "I've been trained that way."

Sam often recounts his experiences of being in the Marine Corps. Boot camp, as other Marines know, is one that tests the limits of your strength and tenacity–both physically and mentally. Many don't make it through, but the ones who do have a resilience like no other. The Crucible is a several-day test at the very end of boot camp designed to extend the bounds of one's physical, emotional, and mental endurance. Simulating combat, you are given one very small meal and only a few hours of sleep. Right when you think the simulation is over, the team is typically delivered a new mission requiring everyone to gear up and keep going. Only the strongest see what others would deem as impossible and still push forward. This is where the name "crucible" was established since the meaning of the name is a process that separates worthy silver from other less valuable metals.

I couldn't help but think Sam was cut out for the kind of tenacity required to survive this journey. I had mistakenly thought the interstage experience in between the Stage 1 Norwood and the Stage 2 Glenn operations was our Crucible. It had tested every domain. By the accounts of so many other families going through HLHS palliative surgeries, the Stage 2 Glenn operation opened up many more opportunities we were looking forward to–better eating, fewer meds, more energy, and growth that was otherwise restricted by a small, malfunctioning heart.

"You'll be in and out" was the phrase we had heard from so many nurses and families. How much we were looking forward to this "new" Cillian. Little did I know our true Crucible was yet to come.

It was August 9th at 8pm, 48 hours after his Stage 2 Glenn procedure where everything had gone better than the team had hoped. Cillian was doing tremendously well from a post-op perspective. Sam and I were thinking our prayers to have him home for his six-month birthday that week were being answered. Within those first 48 hours, he had all of his intercardiac lines removed, was extubated and breathing on his own, and otherwise looked well. We were hours from going to the step-down unit, which was a huge step in the right direction. This was where, as our cardiologist put it, you stay when you are "on your way out of the door." They don't send kids here until they felt they were safe and healthy enough to go home.

Seeing this as being the last night of Sam and I getting rest before we were near leaving the hospital, we decided to go home to get some sleep. There was one instruction we left to the nurse: "Give me a call if Cillian goes to step down early tonight and I will come in to settle him." We rocked him to sleep, gave him a kiss, and walked home in good spirits, thinking about the huge success of the Stage 2 Glenn operation going seamlessly well. After months of nothing but somber melodies that carried us through his interstage, I heard an old familiar tune play softly in the distance. Yes, I recognized that sound. It was the one that reminded me of life's sweetest moments. I hadn't heard these notes since before his diagnosis, when life was going well. Its melody brought a sigh of relief with the thought of his heart getting stronger, of us getting semblances of a "normal" baby experience. *Is recovery really going this well? Did we really get through the interstage period relatively unscathed?* I thought, cautiously. It was almost too good to be true. I disregarded the hesitation and lingered on each note as its tune lulled me to sleep, dreaming of taking Cillian home in a few days time and this nightmare of him being so critical being over.

I woke up to a phone call at 3am from Boston Children's. My mind raced to the request I had made to the nurses for them to call me if he was transferred to another room. *He must have gone to step down*, I thought before I answered, quite excitedly.

"Brynne, this is the ICU attending. I am really sorry to deliver this news, but Cillian had a cardiac arrest. His heart stopped beating for a total of 31 minutes. Since we had difficulty reviving him we had to place him on a life support system called ECMO that externally beats his heart for him. How soon can you and your husband come in?"

The sweet melodies that filled my mind as I fell asleep instantly evaporated, nowhere to be found. And it was here, life's symphony abruptly stopped.

Some say that in traumatic events they black out or forget. There are days I wish my body had responded that same way, but I remember every detail of the next 48 hours. Every look of pity thrown my way by the nurses as we rushed to the conference room and waited for the doctors to explain what had happened. The cortisol that pulsed through my veins left me in a state of shock and panic. The war within myself every second of the next few hours between keeping it together for Sam and Cillian and crumbling from the weight of what just happened. It felt like one of those nightmares that you wake up from in a sweat and breathe a sigh of relief once you realize it was just a dream. Only it wasn't a dream.

Sam and I didn't issue a single word to each other. We just sat in the quiet of the night, speechless and numb, while waiting for the team to come in. *Wake up, Brynne. It's just a dream. Open your eyes. It'll be over soon.* I kept repeating to myself. No sweet melody. No somber tune. Just paralyzing silence. I felt a million thoughts wanting to ravish my brain the minute I would accept what they said happened.

After what seemed like both hours and seconds at the same time, the team came in. "I wish I could tell you what went wrong, but we don't know. Cillian was doing great, then his heart suddenly stopped out of nowhere."

After conducting external compressions they were able to get a faint pulse that would soon soften then stop. Several failed attempts urged the need to open his chest and begin internal compressions while placing him on life support.

As the team relayed the next piece of information, I felt the first fracture of my heart crack with the weight of the news I would next receive. "I want to be honest, you as parents deserve that. Cillian was really difficult to revive. It's likely he lost enough oxygen to the brain to cause significant brain damage. I am so sorry."

My mind raced to the last few innocent moments I had had with him. Of him laughing and smiling. Of him playing and cooing to the sound of my voice. Of him sleeping peacefully in my arms. Was that lost forever? Was that all I got with him? I would have given anything in that moment to go back in time just to relive even a minute of those memories.

The doctor ended on saying one thing that stuck with me. "I know it's a bad situation. But for what it's worth, it's a good thing he was on the ICU and not on the step down unit, which we were about to send him to since he was doing so well. We don't have the life support device ECMO there and the results would have been even more catastrophic. It's also good you didn't stay overnight like you were thinking because I think the trauma of seeing what happened would have scarred you. We see many parents struggle with the effects of witnessing such an event. We also got him on life support in a record time, and with compressions he didn't go longer than a few seconds without oxygen. For a bad situation, a lot of things went well."

I asked the remainder of my questions stoically with a stern and straight face. There was one question I intentionally saved until the end, scared about the answer I would receive.

"Have you seen kids come on and off ECMO without brain injury?" I asked.

"Yes," he replied.

"Is there a chance that could happen for Cillian?" I asked desperately in efforts to keep the hope that I would get my Cillian back.

He looked up from the ground and stared straight into my eyes. They swam with nothing but remorse.

"I wouldn't expect that for Cillian," he replied.

This answer was a gust of wind extinguishing the little flame of hope I had that the Cillian we said goodbye to just ten hours prior would be the same child.

I crumbled into a puddle of tears. And for the first time in my life, I wept. Not cried. Wept. In that moment, I accepted what I had hoped was a nightmare as my new life. And the wall holding back the questions that would shake my faith to its core came flooding in. A distant, angry tune floated in the recesses of my mind. Its sound grew louder as I felt my heart slowly shatter. How could this happen? What does this mean? Can I survive this heartache?

I felt this was the part of the Crucible in boot camp where you think you are near the end–not because someone told you the mission had been accomplished, but by the sheer measurement of your strength. When you know there is no possible way you could push beyond this point. It had to be over. And right as you entertain the thought of sleep and rest, you get new orders. Right as your knees are shaking from fatigue, you have to find the strength to get up and keep on trudging on with a larger mission in mind.

This was our Crucible.

The Stage 2 Glenn was supposed to be easy. Cillian was supposed to be better. He was pegged to go home in a few days time. We had his six-month-old celebration in mind. To be honest, Sam and I barely crossed the interstage line. And right at the place we once thought was the end of our Crucible, we were slapped with the reality that the heart of our Crucible was yet to come.

Sam and I went to the chapel. We stared into the darkness for a good while. It was silent. In the quiet I remembered our wedding day. When engaged, we chose a song to sing at our ceremony that would become our family hymn. In every significant event, both good and bad, we promised to sing this song as a reminder to give thanks to the Lord for the hope given to us through salvation that extends far beyond the events themselves. As an attempt to cling to this promise, I began singing a broken tune.

"My hope is built on nothing less…" the tears flowed down as I sang a shaky tune.

Hope? What hope? I thought.

"….then Jesus' blood and righteousness…" I lost strength to mutter the words and resorted to humming. Over and over I hummed through a veil of hot tears until I found the strength to say the words.

"In every high and stormy gale, my anchor holds within the veil."

Does it? Will it hold this time? I thought to myself.

"When darkness tries to hide His face, I rest on His unchanging grace."

How do I find His 'unchanging' grace with this? Where was His grace when an innocent baby's heart stopped beating? My thoughts continued to pound my mind.

Sam decided to join. We finished singing and took out our Bibles. This was the last thing we wanted to do. I was angry. I was tired. I was bitter. I was afraid. I was hopeless. But despite that, I decided to lay it all at the foot of the cross for the moment.

"Lord, what do You want me to read?" I asked defiantly.

"The story of Abraham and Isaac," he replied.

I flipped to Genesis 22.

We read the passage together out loud. A few things stood out this time given our circumstance.

The passage begins with "the Lord tested Abraham." (Genesis 22:1)

"Abraham" the Lord says.

"Here I am." Abraham replies.

"Take your son, your only son whom you love and offer him on the mountain that I choose for you." (Genesis 22:2)

Abraham must have had similar thoughts to Sam and I. *Why? Why so young? Why put me through this?* Like Abraham, I felt God chose for us a mountain, then instructed the three of us to climb it. A climb that was perilous and seemingly ended in nothing but loss. A climb I didn't want to make.

In the dark of the night in the chapel I asked God, *what do You want from me?* And in that story, He showed me.

"I need you to trust. I need you to surrender." I gently heard.

Abraham climbs the mountain with his son and preps the sacrifice. (Genesis 22:6)

Isaac asks, "Father, you have prepped the sacrifice, but where is the lamb?" (Genesis 22:7)

"The Lord will provide, my son." (Genesis 22:8)

Just as he is about to plunge the knife into his only son, the Lord cries out to Abraham.

"Abraham!" (Genesis 22:11)

"Here I am, Lord." The same response he had when the Lord first called him. Before he knew the cost of answering. One of total surrender. One of complete trust.

"Abraham, I know now that you fear me. I have provided to you a sacrifice. There is a lamb in the thicket. Because you have not withheld your son from me, your only son whom you love, you will be blessed. And I will make your descendants as numerous as the stars in the sky." (Genesis 22:15-18)

To this day the mountain is still called Moriah, whose name means "The Lord will provide."

God one day would sacrifice His own Son whom He loved just as Abraham loved Isaac. Just like the love that Sam and I shared with Cillian. God knew the cost, because He would one day pay it with His own Son, Jesus. God knew Abraham's pain intimately. God knew exactly what He was asking Abraham to do. Yet Abraham chose to trust. Chose to surrender.

And there I was, comforted with the reminder that He is the only One who knows our pain. And as the thick nails plunged into His hands and feet, Jesus looked to this very day. He saw Sam's and my suffering. He felt the effects of a sinful world, a world He did not intend. And His heart broke with ours. Every tear I've cried, Christ and our Heavenly Father have once cried before for us.

God's message to me was clear: I needed to trust. I needed to surrender.

Chapter 6 Devotional

From Grief to Glory

When I found out I was pregnant I bought a Bible that would soon be Cillian's first Bible. In the months leading up to delivery, I would pray for wisdom through the words I would read and notes I would write to him. While I didn't know Cillian's life journey, God did. And I prayed that in every challenge and obstacle he faced, Cillian would turn to the Word knowing that every answer lies in these pages. I prayed for insight and knowledge as I read and took notes that would one day help him in every stumbling block he experienced in life.

Tuesday, one day before we received the initial diagnosis, I had finished reading John and was looking for another book to start and landed in Job. Having read Job several times, I was familiar with the broad overall message, but not the particular insight I gathered. On top of the title page before I started reading, I put a note for Cillian, "This is a great book about how to praise God through tragedy, when all you want to do is turn your back. You are not promised a problem-free life, but you are promised a God who will guide you through and give you peace amongst the storm."

At the time, I didn't know the significance of those words and how they would be more helpful to me than Cillian in the coming year.

Job was a righteous man in God's eyes who God blessed both spiritually and materially with bountiful wealth (Job 1:1). As Satan was roaming the Earth his eyes fixated on Job and he told God, "Does Job fear God for nothing? Have You not made a hedge around him, around his household, and around all that he has on every side?...Stretch out Your hand and touch all that he has, and he will surely curse You to Your face!" (Job 1:9-11)

God tested Job's faithfulness and allowed (a key word) calamity to strike Job. He lost his property, his children, and shortly his health. Job plunged into a deep well of grief and in efforts to help, three of his friends came to his aid: Eliphaz, Bildad, and Zophar (Job 2:11). In his grief, Job claimed his righteousness should have barred him from suffering (Job 32:1). That God had found fault with an innocent man and was therefore unjust and wrong in His ways (Job 31). Job stated he was being unfairly punished by God (Job 9:22). His three friends attempted to combat these claims, but their arguments failed to prove Job wrong. As Job sunk deeper and deeper into his grief, his friends were running out of things to say.

After Cillian's cardiac arrest, I was asking questions I normally had not ever entertained. When all others were happily prepping their nursery, I was praying every day for the Lord to keep Cillian's heart viable during pregnancy. When many were enjoying the newborn scrunch and post-partum experience in the comfort of their home, I was recovering on a hard hospital chair and praying by his bedside every day. Where many were joyfully experiencing newborn milestones, I had to find a way to support Cillian through several near-death experiences and intensive recoveries that robbed him of the ability to laugh, see, and smile for a period of time. How could I be content in that? How could I find joy in that? Like Job, I was counting up the trials I had experienced in life and getting righteous in my spirit, "Lord, was giving me a chronic illness not enough suffering? Was having Cillian go through the 'normal' surgeries not enough? Have I not given You the glory in all of those trials? Why must You give me this continual strife?"

This grief and bitterness turned to jealousy of what I was seeing. I was jealous of my sisters and friends who were going through normal pregnancies. As law students were complaining about workload around me, all I wanted to do was lash out thinking they know about nothing stress and managing work with Sam and I working two full-time jobs out of a hospital bathroom we turned into our "office." I felt entitled and justified in these feelings because of the diagnosis we were given. I felt I had a right to air these complaints given the journey we had to go down.

One of Job's friends named Elihu arrived shortly after the three others, but chose to remain silent until this point of the story (Job 32). He was the youngest there, but God chose him to pour His wisdom over. Elihu became aroused in his anger and began to correct Job on several accounts. Elihu notes that many people turn to God in their strife for a way out, but not as one turns to their Maker who can provide joy in times of trouble (Job 33:26). To pray for God to deliver them from their strife is praying from a heart of pride (Job 35:12). In praying for the Lord to bring joy through the trouble, God promises to restore the afflicted, giving them blessings and watching over them, as He cares for them (Job 42). But even more important than this, Elihu notes that a Godly sufferer who obeys and serves Him will get the ultimate blessing: contentment through the pain (Job 36:11). Elihu corrects Job sternly in saying he should not see his own suffering as God punishing him or as evidence that God has abandoned him. Instead, Job should see this as a way of God humbling Job's spirit, as God teaching Job, and as a way for Job to deepen his relationship with God (Job 40:11).

God Himself, not by a messenger angel, comes down and affirms what Elihu preached. He also says several additional things to Job. First, God illustrates His magnificence and power through nature which He alone orchestrates (Job 38). In this He asks how Job could understand God's ways if he could not comprehend His authority over nature (Job 38:18).

Job recognizes the error in his response to the trials, and repents. He says in his repentance, "I know that You can do everything, and that no purpose of Yours can be withheld from You (Job 42:2)."

In this, God fulfilled His promise to bless those who find peace through the pain by fixing their eyes not on circumstance but on how His glory and power is revealed in such a time. The story ends by illustrating the many ways God blessed Job with even more than he had before tragedy struck (Job 42:16-17).

The answer lies in the core of Job's message, which I recited to myself in waiting for Cillian to arrive: our grief in suffering can also be seen as the magnificent power of God's glory, should we choose to see it.

I have the choice of seeing my having SMA as suffering, or as God's providence so that I would be placed in a high risk OB clinic with specialized technicians skilled enough to catch HLHS the earliest day possible. I have the choice of seeing Sam and I needing to be displaced for a year as suffering, or as God's providence in providing for our every housing, food, and clothing need through Fisher House and other organizations learning about our story. I have the choice of seeing Cillian's cardiac arrest as suffering, or as God's power seen through healing Cillian's brain injury and heart dysfunction when so many doctors prepared us for Cillian to not walk, eat, or talk.

You have the same choices to make. God's promise to reveal Himself to you remains when you are ready to learn about the power of His glory. In practicing this truth, you will quickly learn our joy does not come through circumstance, but in witnessing God's glory through the circumstance in how He tends to those He loves. Whatever may come.

I now read the words I wrote to Cillian with different eyes, "You are not promised a problem-free life, but you are promised a God who will guide you through and give you peace amongst the storm." And He will. I can now go down this road of uncertainty armed with the knowledge of peace that comes through witnessing His power revealed through witnessing His purpose.

Reflection:

1) What is preventing you from God changing your grief and turning it into His glory?

_____

_____

_____

_____

_____

_____

_____

_____

_____

_____

_____

_____

_____

2) What steps can you make in the present to facilitate that transformation?

_____

_____

_____

_____

_____

_____

_____

_____

_____

_____

_____

_____

_____

_____

Finding Joy Through Suffering

Chapter 7

This Side of Heaven

"...but we also glory in tribulations, knowing that tribulation produces perseverance; and perseverance, character; and character, hope. Now hope does not disappoint, because the love of God has been poured out in our hearts by the Holy Spirit who was given to us." - Romans 5:3-5

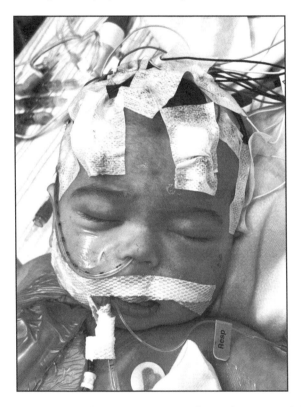

Sam and I were finally able to see Cillian. They warned about tubes and the open chest where we could see his heart beating on life support. What they didn't warn about was the bruising. Signs of people desperate to keep Cillian alive.

I began my scan of the damage. On his wrist I noticed a hard, bumpy bruise.

"What is that?" I asked the nurse.

"Well, Cillian had an IV pulled a few hours before his arrest since he didn't need it and it had clogged. When his heart stopped beating, the body was responding the appropriate way and the blood calcified and hardened."

I could tell she was skirting around the appropriate medical words. Death. Cillian had died for 31 minutes. And the blood thickened as it lost oxygen while the seconds ticked by.

We were told that the next 72 hours were critical, as his body would begin showing signs of brain damage, if there was any. Seconds felt like hours and minutes felt like days as I prayed fiercely for the Lord to heal his brain. Though I felt my faith being shaken, I leaned into it more than ever. In my efforts, I filled my mind with many topics revealing the Lord's power.

I thought about healing, and as I reflected, I prayed, "Lord, You are the great Physician, You give and take away. Please heal this innocent child. Take away the damage that may be there."

I thought of the power of prayer, "Where two or more are gathered, so is He. Delight yourself in the Lord and He will grant you the desires of your heart," it says in Matthew 18:19 and Psalm 37:4. As I reflected on the fact that there were thousands of people praying for the same thing across the world, I was convinced this was going to be a story of God's power in healing. With Cillian being the focus of so many believers and nonbelievers, God just had to show up. What a perfect opportunity to show His power. So I prayed continually for a miracle as I remained desperate to keep the hope that Cillian didn't suffer any brain injury alive. I could feel the jovial melody buried in my mind desperate to come out in celebration with Cillian's healing. Its faint presence motivated me to pray as I had never prayed before.

One day went by. Two days went by. And by 56 hours post-arrest I began to believe the prayer I'd been praying had come true, and we had dodged a very large bullet.

The 60th hour went by and I was giving Cillian a foot rub. As I stretched out his heel, it began to shake. Time froze and my face went pale as I closed my eyes recalling a conversation with a neurologist that echoed in my mind.

"The most common early signs of brain injury would be something called clonus. This is when you push the foot up and it begins to tremor, like a shaking movement." His last word echoed in my mind as I drifted back to reality.

I opened my eyes to Cillian's wobbling foot resting in my hands. I drifted my gaze up to Cillian. His eyes were wide open, his pupils fully expanded. His body was completely contracted.

Time sped back up and I voiced to the nurse urgently, "Page the neurologist, Cillian is seizing."

Within the next five minutes, Cillian's convulsions got worse and worse. I knew what I was seeing. I knew it was seizures. I knew it was signs of brain damage from the cardiac arrest. But I had a deeper understanding beyond that as I knew what this meant for my faith. For the first time in my life, I felt it fracture. The somber melody was suddenly replaced with a cacophony of vexing dissonant sounds as my thoughts began to spiral.

How could God not grant the healing thousands are praying for?

How could God allow a random arrest with unknown origins to the most innocent baby?

How could God not use this as a story to show the millions watching of His goodness, His power, His ability to heal?

But those weren't even the worst thoughts. As I stared into my son's eyes that no longer recognized me, as I saw the bruises marked by efforts to save his life, as I saw tubing and wiring that took up more space on his body than I could see, as I looked at his heart beat artificially through a thin, see-through sterile sheet, I asked myself–*why even save him, God? Why return Cillian to this side of heaven? Why make him suffer even more?* I thought of the lesson He taught me in the chapel, to trust Him and surrender. *Is this what you are commanding me to do Lord? To surrender Cillian in the form of death?*

My prayers changed with these thoughts and images of suffering. *Lord, take his life if it means less pain, if it means he'll be in the arms of his Savior, whole and complete. For the sake of my faith in You, have mercy.*

The thoughts seemed to overpower what little hope I had left to cling to.

Why even pray, Brynne? What's the point? You've prayed before. Where is your God now? Why does He seem silent?

The questions deepened even as the seizures got worse by the hour. The dissonant sounds of life's symphony grew louder and more chaotic with each thought. The notes, deep in vibration, seemed to rattle my heart with every question.

Do I surrender the one I love to a God who allows this to happen? Was my trust in God only when things were going well for Cillian? Was my love for God conditional on Cillian's success?

The further I questioned, the further my heart broke. I felt like a skydiver, once gracefully gliding through the air, slammed by an unexpected gust of wind. Now here I was, in an uncontrollable freefall.

It took four hours to control the seizures. For four hours all I could do was hold the hand of the baby I was laughing with just one week prior. For four hours I felt my heart break and my faith fracture with each second that went by while he convulsed uncontrollably. For four hours I sat there as the above questions mercilessly tortured my mind, heart, and soul.

The neurologist came in later that evening.

"What we saw is concerning. Cillian had been having something called 'subclinical seizures.' This means shortly after he arrested the brain started having seizures that went undiagnosed because of the sedation he was on. Any seizure lasting more than five minutes has the capacity to damage the brain even more. We suspect Cillian had over 12 hours of back-to-back seizures with the longest break in between being ten seconds. What this means for Cillian is a couple things. First, he definitely has a brain injury.

Second, it's extensive. Third, we are worried about Cillian's brain function moving forward."

And then suddenly, the thoughts came to a screeching stop. The music halted abruptly. For the first time since his arrest, my mind went blank. There was no praying. There was no wrestling with God. No melody. Not even dissonance. Then ever slowly, a new and stronger feeling set in. It was anger like I had never felt before. It was bitterness like none other. Just like the song said in the previous chapter.

Several days went by, and Cillian was touch-and-go. His heartbeat slowed several times, necessitating help from an external pacemaker. I wasn't sure if we were planning an extended hospital stay for recovery or a funeral. As the hours ticked by, I felt my spirit hardening. All the while, I knew I was at a crossroads of my own faith and spent significant amounts of time pondering these life-altering questions. I heard the question He had asked me in the chapel repeat over and over, *do you trust me Brynne? Are you willing to surrender what you love most to Me?*

Sleep those days was one thing I begged for, yet was hard to come by. My mom stayed up with me some nights as I rifled through my grief. One thing she said sparked my journey into these questions and spawned the chapters of this very book.

"Don't forget who you are, Brynne. Don't forget who your Creator made you to be and where your joy comes from. And remember, every answer to the questions you have in this life comes from the very Book you want to run the farthest from."

I couldn't tell you what time it was, somewhere in the middle of a long, long night. I was in the room alone with Cillian. Just us two, the machines, and the deafening silence from God.

And then I knew. This was the moment when I would answer the question God had asked me in the chapel. *Do you trust Me, Brynne? Do you surrender Cillian to My will?* echoed in my mind. I whispered every so softly, "Okay, Lord. Cillian is in your hands. I'm choosing to trust. I'm choosing to surrender. Do with him what you will, but protect my heart in the process."

I knew what I was praying for and the ramifications. It was the same as Abraham's prayer surrendering his son, Isaac. It's easy to say you trust in the Lord, but when it could cost you the thing you love most, it's much harder.

But then, in the dead of night as I whispered those words, I felt one thing I hadn't since Cillian had arrested. Peace. I had finally reached a place of surrender. Whether my son would live or die, I was at peace with God's plan.

I took that peace with me into the difficult days ahead. My mom's challenge sparked a deep desire to answer questions about my relationship with God in ways I never had before:

How do I redefine my understanding of God's goodness, mercy, and grace through suffering?

How do I rediscover joy in the face of tragedy?

How do I reconcile God's love for us while allowing the unimaginable to occur?

In my attempts to discover the answers of these questions, I slowly began to see that I had mistaken a fracture of faith for a facet of faith being made, like a diamond made under pressure. I see now that it wasn't that I was losing my faith, it was that God was taking me somewhere deeper. Somewhere I would have never chosen to go on my own, but a place I gained understanding I could not have comprehended elsewhere.

For it was not God who caused the suffering I was experiencing, but sin. God in His power had created the world sinless, but with free will entwined into the fabric of His creation. Where we once walked intimately with our Creator, the veil of sin soon separated. Some effects of sin are self-induced, while the effects of other sins are felt by innocent bystanders such as Cillian. And while I have felt many days it was easier to blame God for my suffering, I soon came to realize blame was the easy way to resolve the pain. To choose to see your Creator as good through innocent suffering is no easy task, yet because of that it is all the more rewarding. For it is in the time your soul blossoms into faith that you discover true peace, undying joy, and unwavering hope that cannot be supplanted by any one thing this world has to offer.

Ever so slowly, even through my most painful days, as I grew deeper in my relationship with my Creator while investigating the questions above, I began to hear a new and sweeter melody develop. It was different from the one I heard before Cillian's diagnosis, when life was going well. Its sound was richer and more robust. The new composition of notes brought tears to my eyes when I thought about how each heartache had brought me to a deeper understanding of the love our Creator has for us. As soon as this melody softly fell upon my ears, I was gifted with something I thought I had lost forever: peace, contentment, and above all joy. Despite what happens to Cillian. Despite the "new" Cillian we were gifted. This is the power of the hope one cannot supplant with anything in this world, hope that can be only found in our understanding of salvation through Christ.

It is through this journey I wrote the devotionals you have read in this book that once served as my guideposts leading me back to my own faith. I don't know what led you to this book, nor your life journey. But I have personally prayed over each chapter, for the souls coming across these pages, to encourage and instill hope through the understanding only salvation can bring. My deepest prayer is that you come to enter into the relationship your Creator has waiting for you, and that you don't let your suffering bar you from seeing the beauty God has in store for your life.

Chapter 7 Devotional

My Story, My Song

The life story of Frances Jane van Alstyne, more commonly known as Fanny Crosby, serves as the inspiration behind the title of this book. Born in 1820, at just six weeks old, Fanny developed a cold which spread to inflammation of the eyes causing her to go blind. Her father died when she was six months old, leaving her mother and grandmother to care for her. Having lost her sight, they would both recite passages of the Bible to her when she was young. Bringing her much comfort, she began committing these passages to memory. At just eight years old she wrote her first poem entitled "Oh what a happy soul am I" whose words go like this:

> "Oh what a happy soul am I, Although I cannot see.
> I am resolved that in this world, Contented I will be.
> How many blessings I enjoy, That other people don't.
> To weep and sigh because I'm blind, I cannot, and I won't"

Fanny would go on to write over 8,000 hymns and become a household name in the 19th century. Perhaps her most famous song is entitled "Blessed Assurance." The entire hymn displays submission to God's will in every situation, both the good and the bad. This concept alone is very countercultural and difficult for many non-Christians to understand. Fanny goes on to discuss that when we exercise this perfect submission, we are "filled with His goodness," and "lost in His love."

Though Fanny lacked vision, she was able to illustrate through her words a story much greater than her own. Through daily surrender to Christ of the good and the bad, we in exchange are "filled with His goodness," and "lost in His love." God reveals these things through our life story, which He uniquely pens and is the sole Author of. And in this quiet and sweet surrender, we receive a "foretaste of glory….echoes of mercy, and whispers of love," no matter the circumstance, no matter how dire.

I have often wondered about, and many times was jealous of, Fanny's joy present through her suffering. Most days after Cillian's arrest I felt angry and bitter. I thought about the last memories we had of Cillian happy without brain damage. He was playing in his jolly jumper and Sam and I were making him laugh.

How can I be joyful in the presence of a brain injury that robbed the happiness found in that memory? How can I find joy in the arrest when my days are consumed with his care, and his nights are restless while his brain recovers? How can I find joy when he is in heart failure and we wait to see whether he is going to get better or continue to decline? How can I find joy when there is nothing but fear on the horizon of Cillian's life? Fear of death, fear of a life continued in suffering, fear of Sam and I being lifelong caretakers, fear of having future children with the same condition? How can I find joy when we deal with so many of the effects of trauma? How can I find joy when the echoes of Cillian's cries when recovering in the ICU are still burned into my memory? How can I find joy when I am angry about our situation? Do I have a right to be angry? Can I be both angry and joyful?

The Bible has direction on this topic. And what we have learned about joy is plentiful. Read each passage out loud and talk about how each illustrates the lessons described below:

1) To experience joy, you must practice gratitude (Daniel 6:10)

Now when Daniel knew that the writing was signed, he went home. And in his upper room, with his windows open toward Jerusalem, he knelt down on his knees three times that day, and prayed and gave thanks before his God, as was his custom since early days.

2) The source of joy is Jesus' love and salvation (Luke 2:10)

Then the angel said to them, "Do not be afraid, for behold, I bring you good tidings of great joy which will be to all people.

3) Joy and hope are intertwined (Romans 15:13)

May the God of hope fill you with all joy and peace as you trust in him, so that you may overflow with hope by the power of the Holy Spirit.

Reflection:

1) This week, write out a gratitude journal specific to the situation that's bringing you suffering. Reflect and pray on those gratitudes this week.

_____

_____

_____

_____

_____

_____

_____

_____

_____

_____

_____

_____

_____

_____

2) Think about how the story of Isaac is used in the lessons of this book, both in this devotional and the prior chapter, "The Crucible." What big picture lesson do you learn by putting both lessons together?

_____

_____

_____

_____

_____

_____

_____

_____

_____

_____

_____

_____

_____

_____

Afterword

Cillian still remains on this side of heaven, a healthy happy one year old. As I write these words, I am sipping coffee to the image of him playing with Sam on the living room floor. Flashes of the many conversations we have had with Cillian's care team while he was in his recovery post-cardiac arrest race through my mind. "Are you sure the report you gave us was accurate?" is a question we receive all too often. Of course they are referring to his MRI revealing moderate brain damage not matching the miraculous healing they were seeing.

I peer deeply into Cillian's eyes, the same eyes that once lacked recognition of who I was because of the brain injury. I cradle him in my arms as I did the night before his Stage 1 Norwood operation, praying for him to survive, only this time he squeals with delight and laughter. I smother him in kisses, the same kisses I gave to him before he had his cardiac arrest and our lives changed forever, only this time he bursts into giggles.

Yes, I recognize this musical theme. It was the one I heard before the diagnosis when everything was going well. I hear that same melody, only it's strengthened by a new tune reflecting the many lessons forged from the fire. This new melody composes themes of peace and joy through tragedy, of life beyond the grave, and hope through the greatest act of selfless love known to mankind through Jesus's sacrifice. This new melody together paired with the old dance around one another creating the perfect harmony.

I choose to listen to this song differently. I close my eyes and cement each memory as I ruminate on every sound I hear. The random bursts of Cillian's laughter. The tenderness of never-ending smiles. In the backdrop of the suffering we just experienced, this music is all the richer, all the sweeter to my ears. How I wish I could freeze this time, wishing our lives could embody this scene forever. But we know deep down that isn't the case for our Cillian.

Only 40% of children with HLHS survive to their fourth birthday.[5] A significant portion of these children will need a heart transplant at some point in their life. Many die waiting.[6] We also know Cillian has his Stage 3 Fontan operation in the near future as he approaches his second birthday. And so, the somber symphonic tunes are bound to return once more. But even still, though the storm lies on the horizon, I rest on the truth that is promised to us through our Savior. Through the darkest of days that could be yet to come, His promise to be present through the pain will give the constant love we need to see us through.

I now understand His goodness to extend beyond the trials we have yet to see through the hope salvation brings, which was

[5]https://pubmed.ncbi.nlm.nih.gov/263919366
[6]https://www.ncbi.nlm.nih.gov/pmc/articles/PMC2715462

gifted to us by His Son. Through the greatest act of love, our Creator sent His only Son who chose to exchange His crown in heaven for a crown of thorns as He freely sacrificed His own life for our gain. And because the veil of sin was separated in this single act alone, we have everlasting hope of being reunited with Him once again. With this promise there is no fear of death. With this promise we are assured eternal life beyond the grave.

I think about the conversation I had with God after Cillian's cardiac arrest. *Do you trust Me, Brynne? Are you willing to surrender the thing you love most for Me?* As I reflect on that question, I think of how my saying "yes" to that question has allowed Cillian's story to reach the masses. I think of how, through his story, awareness about Congenital Heart Defects has reached millions. I think of Sam's and my decision to start Heart Warrior Ministries to help parents and families navigate their "year from hell" with the help they need. I think of the many who have reached out saying how Cillian's story has rejuvenated their own faith in their Creator, and those who have found faith of their own. I think of all these things, then remember Sam's and my first prayer requesting the Lord to use Cillian's story to share the good news of the gospel.

Where many see suffering, I have seen nothing but God's faithfulness. Where many see a story of pain, I have witnessed a journey of peace. Where many have seen a limited life, I see a life full of blessing. This is the power of the God I serve, to turn even the worst parts of life resulting from sin into a beautiful symphony displaying His power and goodness.

Though life has a way of taking me through melodic highs and somber lows, His providence, His presence, and His promise serve as the ever-constant rhythm that supports them all. The sweet new melody I have gained through this experience reminds me of the true joy and peace I have through my Creator, despite what happens. Whether we are gifted more days such as these of Sam and Cillian laughing together on the living room floor, or the image of us standing together in front of a child's casket, I can rest assured there will be no more silence as I once heard in the ICU. Only the faint presence of the melodic tune reminding me of hope that lies beyond the grave, true peace gained through the knowledge of salvation, and undying joy that rests in my relationship with my Creator seeing me through these highs and lows.

This is my story, this is my song. How I pray you come to hear the same tune.

And that is why, I will say till my dying breath, that:

God is good. All the time.

Acknowledgements

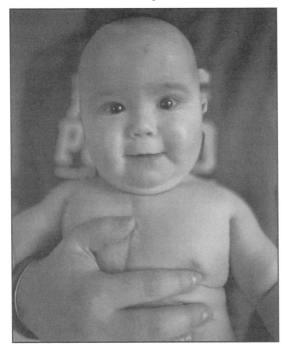

Thank you to my ever-faithful and loving husband, **Sam**, who has never failed to support my wildest dreams. As I sunk endless hours into composing the words in this book, he sacrificed his time willingly to allow me the space to write the words you have just read. In my doubt, he reminded me of the first prayer we prayed upon hearing the diagnosis, that God would use Cillian's story, whatever it may turn out to be, to reveal the mystery and power of God and the hope brought through salvation. He is more than my husband. He is my spiritual rock, mentor, counselor, and best friend. Thank you, my love.

Thank you to my parents, **Amy and Randy Willis**. In the midst of my suffering, in my darkest of days, they reminded me to lean into my relationship with my Creator, not run from it. It was this simple reminder that sparked the discovery of the 'facets of faith' you have read in this book to help others cling to their faith through their suffering.

Thank you to my twin brother and sister in law, **Zach and Caroline Willis**, who have been my lifeline of support throughout this journey. They perfectly exude the example of love that Christ sets by the many sacrifices they have made for Sam, Cillian, and I throughout the ups and downs of this journey. You are so treasured in my heart.

Thank you to my sisters and brother-in-laws, **Jordan and Mallan Clark** and **Nick and Abrielle Ackerman**, who helped support us throughout this journey by dropping everything and helping with logistics and funding for our stay in the hospital.

Thank you to the many nurses at **Boston Children's** who helped Cillian in so many ways. To **Rachael**, thank you for pushing me to see hope when no other doctors could. To **Kim**, thank you for giving me the levelheadedness I needed the many days after Cillian's arrest. To **Christina** who cared for Cillian the day before and after his arrest, thank you for your humor and bright spirit, it is a gift to all who meet you. To **Mary-Magdalene, Aki, Sydney, Heather**, and **Caroline**, thank you for tending to Cillian with all the love and passion you have. To all I have listed and other nurses, thank you for being my friends, my counselors, and my shepherds through my darkest days. You will forever leave an imprint on my heart. May you never get "used to" the daily impact you share with the world that led you to the field. May the hands you have been gifted be healing to all who are honored enough to experience their help.

Finally, I would love to thank **Cillian's prayer warriors** that have sunk hours into the many prayers sent to our Heavenly Father. It was these tens of thousands who sought me through the hardest moments and inspired me to compose these lessons born from such an experience. These words have been written for and in honor of you. May you be blessed tenfold in return.

How You Can Help

Congenital Heart Disease is the most common birth defect to occur, and also one of the most underfunded.[7] This is largely due to a lack of awareness that stymies access to funding for research that leads to treatments and cures. Funding to the below organizations helps support family access to resources and research to help finding cures to conditions like Hypoplastic Left Heart Syndrome.

There are several ways you can help support the cause:

American Heart Association: The AHA's mission is to see a world free of cardiovascular diseases and stroke through funding research and advocacy efforts leading to CHD cures. https://www. heart.org/en/about-us

[7]https://chdcoalition.org/what-we-do/chd-research

American Red Cross: The ARC has officially stated the blood supply is in a critically low state. Throughout his lifetime, Cillian has had up to 20 blood transfusions. It was other people's blood that helped Cillian survive an infection that almost took his life, two emergent open heart surgeries, two planned open heart surgeries, and life support. With critically low blood supplies, the possibility of completing such interventions becomes threatened. In fact, according to the ARC, "blood product distributions to hospitals are outpacing the number of blood donations coming in." Donating your blood to a local Red Cross will help thousands like Cillian get access to the blood they need to survive. To search for your local center, go to the American Red Cross website: https://www.redcross.org/give-blood.html

Congenital Heart Disease Coalition: It is CHD Coalitions ongoing mission to not only directly support research of the disease, but also to unify the CHD community to generate national awareness. This will ultimately help fuel widespread contribution to these research programs. Advocacy leads to funding, which advances research and, ultimately, saves lives. https://chdcoalition.org/what-we-do/chd-research

Fisher House of Boston: Fisher House of Boston's mission is to provide a home away from home where military families can stay, free of charge, while a loved one is receiving in-house treatment at any of our world-renowned medical centers in Boston. While they don't solely focus on CHD, they have supported hundreds of families seeking heart-related treatments in the surrounding Boston area. https://fisherhouseboston.org/

Sisters By Heart: Sisters by Heart is a group of parents and patients who came together during their journeys with Hypoplastic Left Heart Syndrome, many of whom were fortunate to meet prior to their child's birth. We've supported each other in our journeys with single ventricle for the past decade. Knowing the challenges and difficulties we faced at our own child's diagnosis (and those first several months of life), we created Sisters by Heart to reach out and support parents of the newly diagnosed. A major aspect of our mission is sending care packages to parents at the beginning of their journey. We want them to know they are not alone and to provide resources and understanding while their child undergoes care and treatment from birth and beyond. https://www.sistersbyheart. org/who-we-are

Conquering CHD: Originally founded as the Pediatric Congenital Heart Association in 2013, we quickly filled a niche as the voice of the congenital heart patient and family. We are changing both the national landscape and empowering patients and families in their local communities. In 2020, to better reflect our efforts in being more inclusive both culturally and across the lifespan, we changed our name to Conquering CHD. We engage, listen, learn, and act. We create visibility and empower all impacted by CHD. We accomplish this through awareness, community, knowledge, and research. Beginning as a grassroots organization, we have built a robust network of collaborations – patients, family members, lawmakers, medical providers, scientists and media.

Ollie's Branch: Supporting the mental wellness of heart warriors, their families and caregivers is a top priority for Ollie Hinkle Heart Foundation. The stress and challenges heart parents and caregivers face can have significant and lasting effects if not properly addressed. Recent research shows that parents of children with critical congenital heart disease (CHD) are at an elevated risk for mental health problems. Up to 50% report clinically elevated symptoms of depression and/or anxiety and 80% present with clinically significant symptoms of trauma. Ollie's Branch is an access point to mental health specialists that support heart families (including the heart warrior and their parents, siblings, grandparents, and other primary caregivers) through therapy sessions. This program continues to be available to heart families if their heart warrior is now a heart angel. Ollie's Branch is a resource that families can continue to take advantage of throughout their – and their child's – lifetime. https://theohhf.org/ollies-branch/#overview